Klepper

THE INCREDIBLE
SHRINKING ALPHA

Praise for

Swedroe and Berkin provide a concise treatment of the research passive and active investors (both individual and institutional and also financial advisors) need to become more successful. This treatment also appeals to college finance students seeking to gain a better understanding of passive versus active investing, along with "the correct answers." The authors enable investors seeking to "generate real alpha" to understand that passive investing is increasingly the correct approach, while active investing is just the opposite.

— JOHN HASLEM, PROFESSOR EMERITUS OF FINANCE, UNIVERSITY OF MARYLAND, ROBERT H. SMITH SCHOOL OF BUSINESS, AND EDITOR/AUTHOR OF *MUTUAL FUNDS: PORTFOLIO STRUCTURES, ANALYSIS, MANAGEMENT, AND STEWARDSHIP*

Based on decades of research and my personal experiences, I too gave up the quest for alpha long ago. I hold an endowed chair in investments and am a member of The Wall Street Journal Experts panel. Yet, I do not own a single individual stock or corporate bond. Rather, I invest in low-cost passive mutual funds and ETFs. Swedroe and Berkin demonstrate how this strategy can be used to achieve a prudent, globally diversified portfolio. Their book could well end up saving you a lot of money—your money—and giving you a lot of free time.

— WILLIAM REICHENSTEIN, INVESTMENT PROFESSOR AT BAYLOR UNIVERSITY

Ever wonder why your actively managed funds almost invariably disappoint you? Piece by piece, the authors peel back the claims that active managers can add value in a system where it gets harder and harder to generate Alpha. In a world where academic research uncovers the true sources of return and markets relentlessly become more efficient, what's an investor to do? Go passive! Swedroe is the master of explaining financial research in terms that every reader can easily understand. Read and improve your financial acumen.

— FRANCIS ARMSTRONG III, AUTHOR OF *THE INFORMED INVESTOR* AND *INVESTMENT STRATEGIES FOR THE 21ST CENTURY*

In this short but powerful book, Swedroe and Berkin have advanced the debate on active v. passive to a new level. Their discussion of how alpha (beating the market) has steadily morphed into beta (achieving market returns) is the best description I've read of this process yet. No polemics here, just a data centered exposition of the issues—the longtime trademark of Larry Swedroe.

— EDWARD WOLFE, PROFESSOR EMERITUS OF FINANCE, WESTERN KENTUCKY UNIVERSITY

Swedroe and Berkin roll up their sleeves and dig into decades of research to help us better understand how markets work. The result is a clear and concise synthesis of how investing can indeed be a "winner's game." Read, study and apply their approach.

— TOBIAS MOSKOWITZ, FAMA FAMILY PROFESSOR OF FINANCE, UNIVERSITY OF CHICAGO BOOTH SCHOOL OF BUSINESS, AND MANAGING DIRECTOR, AQR CAPITAL MANAGEMENT

The

INCREDiBLE
SHRINKING
ALPHA

The INCREDIBLE SHRINKING ALPHA

SHRINKING

ALPHA

AND WHAT *YOU* CAN DO TO ESCAPE ITS CLUTCHES

LARRY E. SWEDROE & ANDREW L. BERKIN

BAM ALLIANCE Press
8182 Maryland Ave.
Suite 500
St. Louis, MO 63105
thebamalliance.com

Design by Alan Dubinsky

CONTENTS

ACKNOWLEDGMENTS

For all their support and encouragement, Larry thanks his colleagues at Buckingham and the BAM ALLIANCE. He especially thanks his wife Mona, the love of his life, for her tremendous encouragement and understanding during the lost weekends and many nights he sat at the computer well into the early morning hours. She has always provided whatever support was needed. And then some. Walking through life with her has truly been a gracious experience.

Andy thanks his colleagues at Bridgeway Capital Management for their enthusiastic support of this book specifically and his professional and personal life more generally. John Montgomery and Tammira Philippe provided useful feedback on an initial version of the text. Andy also thanks his family, especially his wife Joy and son Evan, for their encouragement and understanding.

Larry and Andy both express their great appreciation for the editorial assistance provided by Nick Ledden, the production assistance of Laura Latragna and the print design from Alan Dubinsky.

CHAPTER 1
THE QUEST FOR
THE HOLY GRAIL

According to legend, the Holy Grail was the dish, plate or cup used by Jesus at the Last Supper. It was believed to possess miraculous powers. Legend has it that the Grail was sent to somewhere in what is now Great Britain, where several guardians keep it safe. The search for the Grail is an important part of the legend of King Arthur and his court.

The financial equivalent of the quest for the Holy Grail is the quest for money managers who *will* deliver alpha, defined as returns above the appropriate risk-adjusted benchmark. For the vast majority of investors, the quest for alpha has been a frustrating one, marked by far more failures than successes. Larry's 2011 book, *The Quest for Alpha: The Holy Grail of Investing*, presented the evidence on the failures of most individual investors, mutual funds, pension plans, hedge funds and venture capitalists to generate alpha over the long run. Unfortunately, as we hope to demonstrate, for those still engaged in that quest, the hurdles to achieving alpha are getting higher and higher. The already low odds of success are persistently shrinking.

We'll begin our story with a discussion of the history of asset pricing models and the important role they play in the quest for alpha.

ASSET PRICING MODELS

Building on the work of Harry Markowitz, the trio of John Lintner, William Sharpe and Jack Treynor are generally given most of the credit for introducing the first formal asset pricing model, the Capital Asset Pricing Model (CAPM). It was developed in the early 1960s.

The CAPM provided the first precise definition of risk and how it drives expected returns. It allowed us to understand whether an active manager who outperforms the market has generated alpha, or whether that outperformance could be explained by exposure to some factor. This is an important issue because active managers charge relatively high fees for the "promise" of alpha. If their outperformance can be explained by exposure to one or more factors—also often referred to as beta, or loading, on the factor—there was no actual outperformance, or alpha, on a risk-adjusted basis. If that is the case, the high fees charged by active managers can no longer be justified. Exposure to various factors can be obtained in a less expensive way through lower-cost vehicles, such as index mutual funds and exchange-traded funds

(ETFs). In other words, if an active manager's above-market performance was due to loading on certain factors, investors paid a high price for alpha but actually received beta. And that exposure can be obtained more cheaply.

THE CAPM: A ONE-FACTOR MODEL

The CAPM looks at risk and return through a "one-factor" lens—the risk and the return of a portfolio are determined only by its exposure to market beta. This beta is the measure of the equity-type risk of a stock, mutual fund or portfolio relative to the risk of the overall market. The CAPM was the financial world's operating model for about 30 years. However, like all models, it was by definition flawed or wrong. If such models were perfectly correct, they would be laws, like we have in physics. Over time, anomalies that violated the CAPM began to surface.

In 1981, Rolf Banz's "The Relationship Between Return and Market Value of Common Stocks" found that market beta doesn't fully explain the higher average return of small stocks. That same year, Sanjoy Basu's "The Relationship Between Earnings' Yield, Market Value and Return for NYSE Common Stocks" found that the positive relationship between the earnings yield (E/P) and average return is left unexplained by market beta. And in 1985, Barr Rosenburg, Kenneth Reid and Ronald Lanstein found a positive relationship between average stock returns and book-to-market ratio (B/M) in their

paper, "Persuasive Evidence of Market Inefficiency." The last two studies provided evidence that, in addition to a size premium, there also was a value premium.

THE FAMA-FRENCH THREE-FACTOR MODEL

The 1992 paper "The Cross-Section of Expected Stock Returns," by Eugene Fama and Kenneth French, basically summarized and explained these anomalies in one place. The essential conclusion from the paper was that the CAPM explained only about two-thirds of the differences in returns of diversified portfolios, and that a better model could be built using more than just the one factor. Fama and French proposed that, along with the market factor of beta, exposure to the factors of size and value explain the cross-section of expected stock returns. The Fama-French model greatly improved upon the explanatory power of the CAPM, accounting for more than 90 percent of the differences in returns between diversified portfolios. From 1927 through 2013, the *annual* average premiums were:

- Beta, defined as the average return of the total U.S. stock market minus the return of one-month Treasury bills: 8.2 percent

- Size, defined as the average return of the smaller half of stocks minus the average return of the larger half: 3.1 percent

- Value, defined as the average return of the highest 30 percent of stocks as ranked by B/M minus the average return of the lowest 30 percent: 4.9 percent

Prior to the development of the three-factor model, actively managed funds could produce higher returns than a benchmark, such as the Russell 3000 Index or the S&P 500 Index, by "tilting" their portfolio to either small stocks or value stocks, thus giving them more exposure to the size and value factors than the benchmark index. The fund would then claim that its outperformance was, in fact, alpha. Today, regression analysis would show that their outperformance was simply the result of a greater exposure to certain factors. In effect, what once was alpha had now become beta, or loading on a factor, which could be purchased in a less expensive way.

With the inclusion of the value premium the three-factor model went a long way toward explaining the superior performance of the superstar investors from the value school of Benjamin Graham and David Dodd. The anomaly these investors presented became less as alpha transformed into beta (loading on factors). Of course, this shouldn't detract from how we should view the ingenuity of their work. After all, they employed these strategies before factors were added to the model. But, we aren't yet done in shrinking alpha.

MOMENTUM FACTOR ADDED CREATING FOUR-FACTOR MODEL

In 1997, Mark Carhart, in his study "On Persistence in Mutual Fund Performance," was the first to use momentum, together with the Fama-French factors, to explain mutual fund returns. Momentum was initially published by Jegadeesh and Titman in 1993 and here is defined as the last 12 months of returns, excluding the most recent month. The momentum factor is the average return of the top 30 percent of stocks minus the average return of the bottom 30 percent as ranked by this measure. This new momentum factor made another significant contribution to the explanatory power of the model. For the period from 1927 through 2013, the *annual* average return to the momentum factor was 8.4 percent.

Since 1998, the four-factor model has been the standard tool used to analyze and explain the performance of investment managers and investment strategies. And once again, alpha had become beta—or loading on a factor as the way to explain returns. Again, it is important to remember that this doesn't take away anything from the active managers who were exploiting the momentum factor before academics added it to the model.

A recent contribution to the model, and one that helps further explain Warren Buffett's superior performance, is from Robert Novy-Marx. His June 2012 paper, "The Other

Side of Value: The Gross Profitability Premium," provided investors with new insights into the cross-section of stock returns. Marx found that profitable firms generate significantly higher returns than unprofitable ones, despite having significantly higher valuation ratios.

Controlling for profitability, here defined as revenues minus cost of goods sold divided by assets, increases the performance of value strategies, particularly when value is defined by book-to-market. The most profitable firms earn average returns that are 3.7 percent per year higher than the least profitable firms. This idea has been extended to a quality factor, which captures a broader set of quality characteristics. In particular, high-quality stocks that are profitable, stable, growing and have a high payout ratio outperform low-quality stocks with the opposite characteristics. And once again, alpha has become beta.

Still, there remain anomalies that these factor models cannot explain. Kewei Hou, Chen Xue, and Lu Zhang, authors of the September 2012 study, "Digesting Anomalies: An Investment Approach," proposed a new four-factor model (market beta, size, investment and profitability) that went a long way to explaining many of the anomalies. An updated version has been accepted for publication in the *Review of Financial Studies*.

The authors defined their investment factor as the difference between the return on a portfolio of low investment-to-assets stocks and the return on a portfolio of high investment-to-assets stocks. They explain: "Intuitively, investment predicts returns because given expected cash flows, high costs of capital imply low net present values of new capital and low investment, and low costs of capital imply high net present values of new capital and high investment." They noted that the investment factor is highly correlated (0.69) with the value premium, suggesting that this factor plays a similar role to that of the value factor. The investment factor earned a highly significant average return of 0.45 percent per month. (Because of its ability to eliminate many anomalies this new four-factor model, which the authors named the q-factor model, may offer a compelling alternative to the Fama-French four-factor model as the workhorse asset pricing model. For that reason, a more detailed explanation of the model can be found in Appendix F.)

As the Digesting Anomalies study shows, research on the definition, characteristics and interplay between factors continues to evolve. For some of these factors, such as size and value, investment companies offer a number of strategies explicitly delivering this exposure. For other factors, firms are adjusting the portfolio construction rules in order to increase exposure. With greater understanding and greater adoption, we see that alpha is continuing to become beta. The result is that the available pool of potential sources of alpha keeps shrinking. The best demonstration of how alpha becomes beta can be found in the study "Buffett's Alpha."

EXPLAINING BUFFETT'S ALPHA

The "conventional wisdom" has always been that Warren Buffett's success can be explained by his stock-picking skills and his discipline—his ability to keep his head while others are losing theirs. However, the 2013 study "Buffett's Alpha," authored by Andrea Frazzini, David Kabiller and Lasse H. Pedersen, provides us some interesting and unconventional answers. The authors found that, in addition to benefiting from the use of cheap leverage provided by Berkshire's insurance operations, Warren Buffett bought stocks that are safe, cheap, high-quality and large. The most interesting finding in the study was that stocks with these characteristics tend to perform well in general, *not just the stocks with these characteristics that Buffett buys.*

High-quality companies have the following traits: low earnings volatility, high margins, high asset turnover (indicating efficiency), low financial leverage, low operating leverage (indicating a strong balance sheet and low macroeconomic risk) and low specific stock risk (volatility unexplained by macroeconomic activity). Companies with these characteristics have historically provided higher returns, especially in down markets.

In other words, it is Warren Buffett's strategy, or exposure to factors, that explains his success, not his stock-picking skills. Andrea Frazzini and Lasse H. Pedersen, the authors of the 2014 study "Betting Against Beta," found that once all the factors—market beta, size, value, momentum, betting against beta, quality and leverage—are accounted for, a large part of Buffett's performance is explained, and his alpha is statistically insignificant.[1]

Again, it is important to understand that this finding doesn't detract in any way from Warren Buffett's performance. After all, it took decades for modern financial theory to catch up with him and discover his "secret sauce." And being the first, or among the first, to discover a strategy that beats the market is what will buy you that yacht, not copying the strategy after it is already well known and all the low hanging fruit has been picked.

With that said, the findings do provide insight into why Warren Buffett was so successful. His genius appears to be in recognizing long ago that these factors work. He applied leverage without ever resorting to a fire sale and stuck to his principles. Buffett himself stated in Berkshire's 1994 annual report: "Ben Graham taught me 45 years ago that in investing it is not necessary to do extraordinary things to get extraordinary results."

---

1. An article by John Alberg and Michael Seckler questioned some of these conclusions, noting, for example, that Buffett looked at different value metrics than B/M, avoided leverage and didn't even have the insurance part of the business until later years. These are valid points, and we are firm believers in using other value metrics such as price relative to earnings and cash flow. But the main point that Buffett uses certain factors still holds, regardless of specific definitions.

BOND INVESTING

We now turn our attention to the world of bonds. Just as we have factor models for stocks, we have them for bonds as well. There are two factors that explain the vast majority of the differences in returns among bond portfolios: term risk (otherwise referred to as duration) and default risk (credit).

From 1926 through 2013, the annual average term premium was 2.4 percent and the annual average default premium was just 0.3 percent. These factors are referred to as risk factors, and have earned premium returns as compensation for the incremental risks of their purchase. Note though that historically, taking credit risk has not been well rewarded, especially after costs (the premium has been just 0.3 percent before implementation costs). Thus, actively managed bond funds could expect to outperform their benchmark, such as the Barclay's Aggregate Bond Index, by tilting their portfolios to achieve more exposure to these factors. And when the funds outperformed, they would claim alpha. With the two-factor bond model, we can now determine whether returns are truly alpha, or simply exposure to the factors. And, as is the case with equity factors, exposure to bond factors can be achieved through low-cost, passively managed vehicles.

The bottom line is that the factor models not only have advanced our understanding of what drives the risks and expected returns of portfolios, but also enable us to separate

alpha from beta. That, in turn, allows you to avoid paying the high fees of active management for delivering beta.

There is another important insight that we need to cover. Doing so allows us to relate one of our favorite stories.

THE TWENTY DOLLAR BILL

There is an old story about a financial economist who also happened to be a passionate defender of the efficient markets hypothesis (EMH). He was walking down the street with a friend. The friend stops and says: "Look, there is a $20 bill on the ground." The economist turns and says: "Can't be. If there was a $20 bill on the ground, somebody already would have picked it up." This joke is told by those who believe that the markets are inefficient, and that investors can outperform it by exploiting mispricings. The market equivalent of finding that $20 bill is finding an undervalued stock. However, the comparison to the EMH in this joke is actually misleading. The following version is a much better one.

A financial economist, and a passionate defender of the EMH, was walking down the street with a friend. The friend stops and says: "Look, there is a $20 bill on the ground." The economist turns and says: "Boy, this must be our lucky day! Better pick that up quickly because the market is so efficient it won't be there for long. Finding a $20 bill lying around happens so infrequently that it would be foolish to spend our time searching for more of them. Certainly, after assigning a value to the time spent in the effort, an 'investment' in trying to find money lying on the street just waiting to be picked up would be a poor one. I am certainly not aware of anyone who has achieved wealth by 'mining' beaches with metal detectors or scouring sidewalks." When he had finished they both looked down and the $20 bill was gone!

There is also what might be called "The Hollywood Version" of this story. A financial economist, and a passionate defender of the EMH, was walking down the street with a friend. The friend stops and says: "Look, there is a $20 bill on the ground." The economist turns and says: "Can't be. If there was a $20 bill on the ground somebody already would have picked it up." The friend bends down and picks up the $20 bill and dashes off. He then decides that this is an easy way to make a living. He abandons his job and begins to search the world for $20 bills lying on the ground, just waiting there to be picked up. A year later, the economist is walking down the same street and sees his long-lost friend lying on the sidewalk wearing torn and filthy clothing. Appalled to see the disheveled state into which his friend had sunk, the economist rushes over to find out what had happened. The friend tells that him that, after his first bit of good luck, he never again found another $20 bill.

Those that tell the first version of the story fail to understand that an efficient market doesn't mean that there cannot be a $20 bill lying around. Instead, it means that because it is so unlikely you will find one, it does not pay to go looking for them. The costs of the effort are likely to exceed the benefits. More importantly, if it became known that there were lots of $20 bills to be found in a certain area, everyone would be there competing to find them. That popularity reduces the likelihood of achieving an appropriate "return on investment."

The analogy to the EMH is in the fact that it is not impossible to uncover an anomaly (that $20 bill lying on the ground) that can be exploited (buying a stock that is somehow undervalued by the market). Instead, one of the fundamental tenets of the EMH is that in a competitive financial environment, successful trading strategies self-destruct because they are self-limiting. When they are discovered, they are eliminated by the very act of exploiting the strategy, as investors buying the undervalued asset and selling the overvalued one cause prices to rapidly converge. In fact, as we have been discussing, that is exactly how the "science of investing" advances. While active investors used to be able to claim alpha by loading up on small, value, momentum and quality stocks, they can no longer do so. It's possible that true stock picking skill can be arbitraged away as the technique becomes well known and more people start using it. It's also possible that what could once be considered stock picking skill can transform into nothing more than exposure to certain common factors.

In their 1996 paper, "The Efficient Market Theory Thrives on Criticism," economics professors Dwight Lee and James

Verbrugge of the University of Georgia explained the power of the efficient markets theory in the following manner:

> *The efficient market theory is practically alone among theories in that it becomes more powerful when people discover serious inconsistencies between it and the real world. If a clear efficient market anomaly is discovered, the behavior (or lack of behavior) that gives rise to it will tend to be eliminated by competition among investors for higher returns. [For example,] if stock prices are found to follow predictable seasonal patterns unrelated to financially relevant considerations, this knowledge will elicit responses that have the effect of eliminating the very patterns they were designed to exploit. The implication here is rather striking. The more empirical flaws that are discovered in the efficient market theory, the more robust the theory becomes. [In effect,] those who do the most to ensure that the efficient market theory remains fundamental to our understanding of financial economics are not its intellectual defenders, but those mounting the most serious empirical assault against it.*

We now turn our attention to another important issue related to that incredibly shrinking alpha. Alpha is a

zero-sum game, meaning that for some investors to generate alpha, they must exploit the mistakes of others.[2]

---

2. Technically speaking, this need not strictly be true. Investors may sell an asset for tax purposes, diversification or risk control, or to raise cash for spending such as in retirement. All these are reasons where investors might not care about being on the winning side of a trade, and they are discussed further in Chapter 4. But these tend to be a small percentage of the total trades and so won't materially affect the outcome. As the amount of trades by institutional investors has grown dominant over the years, the zero sum statement is both broadly true and matched by observed results.

CHAPTER 2
THE POOL OF VICTIMS IS SHRINKING

In his famous 1991 paper, "The Arithmetic of Active Management," Nobel Prize winner William Sharpe explained that before costs active management is a zero-sum game, and after costs it is a negative-sum game: He writes: "Properly measured, the average actively managed dollar must underperform the average passively managed dollar, net of costs. Empirical analyses that appear to refute this principle are guilty of improper measurement." In other words, for active managers to be successful they must have victims that they can exploit. Who exactly are these victims?

The evidence is that the victims are likely to be individual investors. The research has found that, in aggregate, individual investors around the globe underperform standard benchmarks, such as low-cost index funds, even before costs or taxes. When they trade, they are exploited by institutional investors. And while there is a wide dispersion of results among individual investors, even the best traders have a hard time covering costs. Interestingly, research by Brad Barber and Terrance Odean has found that not all underperformance can be attributed to the excessive trading done by individual investors. On average, individual investors exhibit perverse security selection abilities—they buy stocks that go on to earn sub-par returns and sell stocks that go on to earn above-average returns.

Since alpha is a zero-sum game, if there are losers, even before costs, there must be winners. Who are the winners? The winners are institutional investors, such as actively managed mutual funds. The research shows that on a *gross* return basis, active fund managers are able to generate alpha, exploiting the bad behavior of individual investors. For example, Jonathan Berk and Jules van Binsbergen, authors of the 2013 study "Measuring Skill in the Mutual Fund Industry," found that the average mutual fund has added value by extracting about $2 million per year from financial markets, and that the value added is persistent for as long as 10 years. Berk and van Binsbergen concluded: "It is hard to reconcile their findings with anything other than the existence of money management skill."

The 2000 study, "Mutual Fund Performance: An Empirical Decomposition into Stock-Picking Talent, Style, Transactions Costs, and Expenses" by Russ Wermers, provides further evidence of stock-picking skill. Wermers found that on a risk-adjusted basis, the stocks active managers selected outperformed their benchmark by 0.7 percent per year. However, investors earn net, not gross, returns. The research finds that their total expenses—not just the fund's expense ratio, but trading costs as well—more than eroded the benefits derived from their stock-selection skills, leaving investors with *net* negative alphas. What economists call the "economic rent" is going to the scarce resource (the ability to generate alpha) not to the plentiful resource (investor capital). That occurs just as economic theory predicts it should. But while active institutional investors have been able to exploit the bad behavior of individual investors, the fund sponsors have been the winners, not investors in the funds.

THE TREND IS NOT THE FRIEND OF ACTIVE INVESTORS

Making matters worse is that there are trends working against active investors. As Robert Stambaugh points out in his 2014 study, "Investment Noise and Trends," there has been a substantial downward trend in the fraction of U.S. equity owned directly by individuals. In other words, the pool of victims to exploit is shrinking.

Stambaugh noted that at the end of World War II, households directly held more than 90 percent of U.S. corporate equity. By 1980, U.S. corporate equity directly held by households had fallen to 48 percent. By 2008, it had dropped to around 20 percent. The financial crisis certainly did nothing to alter the trend.

Even within the institutional space, the availability of victims to exploit is shrinking. Thirty years ago, almost all mutual funds were actively managed.

Today, index funds account for almost 20 percent of the industry, and their share is steadily growing. For example, in 2013, $3.4 billion flowed into active funds while index-based strategies pulled in more than $60 billion. The fraction of institutional assets in passive funds is growing fast as well. By 2006, the amount of institutional assets in actively managed funds was already below 60 percent.

One logical explanation for the rapid decrease in the active share of the institutional market is that institutional investors are more likely to be aware of the academic literature demonstrating just how difficult a game active management is to win. Another possible explanation is that they are also aware that the pool of victims available to exploit is rapidly shrinking, raising the hurdles for successful active management.

Making matters worse is that while the pool of victims has been shrinking, the competition seeking to exploit pricing mistakes has increased dramatically. There are now more than 7,500 mutual funds, according to the Investment Company Institute. That is 14 times more than there were in 1979. The increased competition for a limited amount of alpha reduces the ability of any given fund to outperform.

The increased competition isn't coming just from actively managed mutual funds. In less than 10 years, the amount of capital invested in hedge funds has increased from about $1 trillion to almost $3 trillion. And with institutional investors now doing as much as 90 percent of the daily trading, who exactly are the victims these sophisticated investors are going to exploit in their quest for alpha? In the zero-sum game (negative-sum after costs) that institutional investors are playing, the other side of the trade is highly likely to be another institutional investor—and only one of the two can be on the right side of a transaction.

The results of a study on the performance of the Yale Endowment provides us with an illustration of just how tough is the competition for alpha.

THE SUCCESS OF THE YALE ENDOWMENT

David Swensen has been the chief investment officer of the Yale Endowment Fund since 1985. He has authored two books we highly recommend, *Pioneering Portfolio Management* and *Unconventional Success*. Because of the success of Yale's Endowment Fund—it generated a 20-year annualized return of 15.6 percent for the period ending in fiscal 2007, a 3.8 percentage points per year higher return than provided by the S&P 500 Index—Swensen is one of the most respected investment managers in the world. But, until recently, very little was known about the reasons behind those stellar returns.

Was Yale's success a result of manager skill or exposure to risk? Or perhaps it was a lucky random outcome?

Peter Mladina and Jeffery Coyle sought to answer that question in their study, "Yale's Endowment Returns: Manager Skill or Risk Exposure," which was published in the summer 2010 edition of *The Journal of Wealth Management*. The following is a summary of their findings:

- In regard to Yale's public equity holdings, returns are fully explained by exposure to factors, not manager skill in picking stocks. Excess returns over their chosen benchmark, the Wilshire 5000, were achieved by the endowment fund's exposure to small-cap and value stocks. A similar result was found internationally. While the endowment did beat its benchmark, the Morgan Stanley Capital Index (MSCI) EAFE (Europe, Australasia and the Far East) Index, the outperformance was explained by exposure to emerging market stocks and the same Fama-French risk factors. In other words, the benchmarks were inappropriate.

- The private equity managers Yale hired did add value. Note that private equity is the one asset class or investment category in which there is some evidence of persistence in performance. This is not true for hedge funds.

The implication is that it has been the endowment's private equity exposure—venture capital in particular—that is the unique source of its excess return.

The authors found the same results when they studied just the last 10 years of the 20-year period ending in fiscal 2007. They concluded that, while the conventional wisdom has held Yale's success is attributable to their ability to hire top active investment managers, the fund's returns can actually be explained by consistent exposure to diversified, risk-tilted, equity-oriented assets and extraordinary outperformance in private equity and venture capital in particular. Outside of private equity, the endowment appeared to underperform risk-adjusted benchmarks.

The authors concluded that any disciplined investor with a high risk tolerance could replicate Yale's results using publicly available index funds and some degree of leverage. The implication is striking. If Yale, with all of its resources, could not generate alpha in publicly traded securities, the competition must surely be very tough indeed.

The findings of this study are supported by the results of the broader 2013 study on university endowments, "Do (Some) University Endowments Earn Alpha?" The authors, Brad Barber and Guojun Wang, analyzed the performance of a large set of institutions over the 21 years ending in June 2011. The following is a summary of their findings:

- A simple factor model (which did not include

the size and value factors) showing a 59 percent exposure to stocks (the S&P 500 for U.S. stocks and MSCI ex-U.S. for international stocks) and a 41 percent exposure to bonds (Barclays Capital Aggregate Bond Index) explains virtually all (99 percent) of the returns.

- Even before adjusting for exposure to small and value stocks, the endowments' small positive alpha of 0.4 percent per year wasn't statistically different from zero. And—given that in the U.S. the size premium was about 2.6 percent per year and the value premium was about 4.5 percent per year over the period studied—it seems likely that if returns were adjusted to account for exposure to small and value stocks, alpha would have been zero or negative.

- Despite taking on more risks in the form of opaque investments (such as hedge funds), and lack of liquidity (in hedge funds and private equity), there was no evidence that the average endowment is able to deliver alpha relative to public stock or bond benchmarks.

It is important to note that the authors reached this conclusion despite recognizing that their data could contain a positive bias resulting from the voluntary nature of reporting. "If institutions are reluctant to publicize poor performance, they may refrain from reporting in below-par years and the reported returns would overestimate the performance of endowments."

THE GOOD NEWS

While the news on the ability to generate alpha is not heartening, for individual investors who recognize that active management is what Charles Ellis called a loser's game—a game that, while it is possible to win, has odds of doing so that are so low it is not prudent to try—the trends are all favorable. If you are one of these individual investors, you are likely benefiting from the intense competition between providers of passively managed funds. By passive we mean funds that have portfolio construction rules that are based on evidence (not opinions), are transparent, and are implemented in a systematic manner. Competition from the many providers of exchange-traded funds (ETFs), with their lower costs, has been driving expense ratios persistently lower. There are now many index products with fees in the single digits. For example, the Schwab U.S. Broad Market ETF (SCHB) has an annual expense ratio of just 0.04 percent.

The trend to lower expenses is making passive investing even more of a winner's game. And that is contributing to a virtuous circle —lower costs are helping drive more investors to become passive, shrinking the pool of victims that can be exploited and raising the hurdles for the generation of alpha.

There is another insight that we can draw from the trend. It seems likely that those abandoning active management in favor of passive strategies will be investors who have had poor experiences with active investing. Thus, it seems logical to conclude that the remaining players are likely to be the ones with the most skill. After all, if an investor's outperformance was based on good luck, the good luck will eventually disappear and they will abandon the game. As less-skilled investors abandon active strategies, the level of competition among the remaining participants will increase. The following example from game theory helps explain why the level of competition is likely to continue to increase, persistently raising the hurdles for successful active management.

GAME THEORY AND INVESTING

Imagine the following scenario: You are an NBA player. The league is holding a free-throw shooting contest open to all players. Each participating player will take 100 shots, receiving $1,000 for each shot made. You are given a choice to play or not play the game. If you don't play, you will get paid based on the average score of all the players who decide to participate. The best free-throw shooter in the league shoots about 90 percent, the average player shoots just 73 percent and you shoot 83 percent. Should you compete or accept the average score of those who participate?

Since you shoot an above-average percentage, it seems like you should play. However, the fact that you are above average is irrelevant because all those with a below-average shooting percentage should choose not to play. Anticipating this occurrence, even those with above-average scores should decide not to play. Logically, only the player with the best percentage should choose to play, and everyone now has an expected return of $90,000.

What does this scenario have to do with investing? As we have discussed, it seems likely that those abandoning active management in favor of passive strategies will be investors who have had poor experiences with active investing. As less-skilled investors abandon active strategies, the level of competition among the remaining players will increase.

THE PARADOX OF SKILL

What so many people fail to comprehend is that in many forms of competition, such as chess, poker or investing, it is the *relative* level of skill that plays the more important role in determining outcomes, not the *absolute* level. What is referred to as the "paradox of skill" means that even as skill level rises, luck can become more important in determining outcomes if the level of competition is also rising.

Charles Ellis, one of the most respected people in the investment industry, noted the following in a recent issue of the *Financial Analysts Journal*. He wrote that "over the past 50 years, increasing numbers of highly talented young investment professionals have entered the competition... They have more-advanced training than their predecessors, better analytical tools, and faster access to more information." Legendary hedge funds, such as Renaissance Technology, SAC Capital Advisors and D.E. Shaw, hire Ph.D. scientists, mathematicians and computer scientists. MBAs from top schools, such as Chicago, Wharton and MIT, flock to investment management armed with powerful computers and massive databases.

For example, Eduardo Repetto, the co-CEO of Dimensional Fund Advisors (DFA), has a Ph.D. from Caltech and worked there as a research scientist, and DFA's co-CIO Gerard O'Reilly also has a Caltech Ph.D. in Aeronautics and Applied Mathematics. And co-author Andrew Berkin, the Director of Research at Bridgeway Capital Management, has a Caltech B.S. and University of Texas Ph.D. in physics, and is a winner of the NASA Software of the Year award. According to Ellis, the "unsurprising result" of this increase in skill is that "the increasing efficiency of modern stock markets makes it harder to match them and much harder to beat them, particularly after covering costs and fees."

Analogous examples are seen in the sports world. For instance, from the advent of the modern baseball era in 1903, seven players achieved a batting average over .400 a total of 12 times. But the last to do so was Ted Williams, who hit .406 in 1941, more than 70 years ago. Yet, today's players are superior athletes—they are demonstrably bigger, faster and stronger, use superior training techniques and have better diets.

However, *all* players have these advantages. The result is that as average skill increases, it becomes more difficult to outperform by large margins—the standard deviation of outcomes narrows. In the first twenty years of the modern era (1903-1921) the average hitter batted about .250-.260. During that period, the .400 mark was reached four times. Since 1950, batting averages have been fairly stable in that same .250-.260 range. Yet no one has hit .400. Why? While batting averages were the same in the two eras, the standard deviation has dropped dramatically, from 40.6 points in 1921 to 26.1 in 2003. Batting .400 is now more than a five standard deviation event, with a probability of less than one in a thousand in a given year. In other words, no one hits .400 any more because the *average* baseball player of today is far better than the average player of a hundred years ago.

We see similar evidence when looking at basketball. For example, beginning with the 1959-1960 season, Wilt (the Stilt) Chamberlain had three seasons when he averaged more than 25 rebounds a game. He also had 11 seasons in a row when he averaged more than 22. Beginning with the 1957-1958 season, Bill Russell had 10 years in a row when he averaged more than 20 rebounds a game. And beginning with the 1958-1959 season, he had seven in a row when he average more than 23. While there's no doubt that today's professional basketball players are superior athletes to those who competed 50 years ago, the leading rebounder in the NBA last year was DeAndre Jordan, who averaged just 13.6 rebounds per game. And just four players averaged at least 12. Chamberlain also averaged over 50 points per game in the 1960-1961 season. Since then, the highest average by a player not named Chamberlain was the 37.1 points per game achieved by Michael Jordan in the 1986-1987 season. Last year, Kevin Durant led the league with an average of 32 points per game.

The paradox of skill means that while today's athletes are more skillful, they are not likely to produce the kind of outlier results that the legends of yesteryear achieved. We see the same phenomenon in the game of active management, where the quest for alpha has become ever more frustrating as the level of skill among competitors rises.

The 2013 Credit Suisse report "Alpha and the Paradox of Skill" by Michael Mauboussin and Dan Callahan examined the effects of increasing skill in investing. They plotted the rolling five-year average standard deviation of excess returns in U.S. large-cap mutual funds over the last 45 years. You should expect to see wide dispersions when there are large differences in the level of skill. Their plot below, updated through 2013, demonstrates a clear trend of declining dispersion in excess returns, which fits nicely with our narrative indicating that competition is getting tougher.

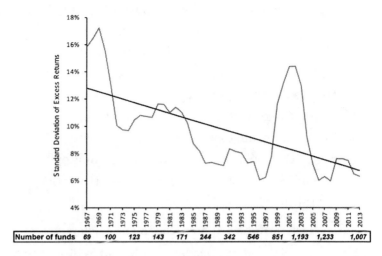

Source: Michael Mauboussin and Dan Callahan, "Alpha and the Paradox of Skill," July 15, 2013.

The study "Conviction in Equity Investing" by Mike Sebastian and Sudhakar Attaluri, which appears in the Summer 2014 issue of *The Journal of Portfolio Management*, provides further evidence of a declining ability to generate alpha. The authors found:

- Since 1989 the percentage of managers who evidenced enough skill to basically match their costs (showed no net alpha) has ranged from about 70 percent to as high as about 90 percent, and by 2011 was at about 82 percent.

- The percentage of unskilled managers has ranged from about 10 percent to about 20 percent, and by 2011 was at about 16 percent.

- The percentage of skilled managers began the period at about 10 percent, rose to as high as about 20 percent in 1993 and by 2011 had fallen to just 1.6 percent. This last result matches closely the result of the 2010 paper, "Luck versus Skill in the Cross-Section of Mutual Fund Returns." The authors, Eugene Fama and Kenneth French, found that only managers in the 98th and 99th percentiles showed evidence of statistically significant skill.

Lubos Pastor, Robert F. Stambaugh and Lucian A. Taylor, authors of the August 2013 paper, "Scale and Skill in Active Management," provided further insight into why the hurdles to generating alpha are getting higher. The authors, whose study covered the period from 1979 to 2011 and more than 3,000 mutual funds, concluded that fund managers have become more skillful over time. "We find that the average fund's skill has increased substantially over time, from -5 basis points (bp) per month in 1979 to +13 bp per month in 2011."[3] However, they also found that the higher skill level has not been translated into better performance. They reconcile the upward trend in skill with no trend in performance by noting: "Growing industry size makes it harder for fund managers to outperform despite their improving skill. The active management industry today is bigger and more competitive than it was 30 years ago, so it takes more skill

---

3. One basis point is one-hundredth of a percent; 100 basis points equals 1%.

just to keep up with the rest of the pack." These findings are consistent with everything we have discussed so far.

The authors also came to another interesting conclusion: the rising skill level they observed was not due to increasing skill within firms. Instead, they found: "The new funds entering the industry are more skilled, on average, than the existing funds. Consistent with this interpretation, we find that younger funds outperform older funds in a typical month." For example, they found: "funds aged up to three years outperform those aged more than 10 years by a statistically significant 0.9% per year." The authors hypothesized that this is the result of newer funds having managers who are better educated or better acquainted with new technology—though they provide no evidence to support that thesis. The authors also found that all fund performance deteriorates with age as industry growth creates decreasing returns to scale and newer, and more skilled, funds create more competition.

Even though the absolute skill level of active managers is increasing, it is getting harder and harder to generate alpha because the level of competition is also increasing. Thus, unless you happen to be Warren Buffett, the winning strategy is to not play. Instead, the winning strategy is to accept market returns in the asset classes, or factors, in which you choose to invest.

But even if you do have Warren Buffett-like skill, the evidence presented in the table below suggests that it is still getting harder and harder to generate alpha.

1999–2013

	15-YEAR ANNUALIZED RETURNS (%)
BERKSHIRE HATHAWAY (BRK)	6.4
S&P 500 INDEX	4.7
MSCI US PRIME MARKET VALUE INDEX	6.2
MSCI US SMALL CAP 1750 INDEX	10.4
MSCI US SMALL CAP VALUE INDEX	10.5
DOW JONES US SELECT REIT INDEX	10.5
EQUAL-WEIGHTED INDEX PORTFOLIO	8.5

The table shows the performance of Berkshire Hathaway (BRK), along with the return of the S&P 500 Index and four domestic asset class indices (large value, small, small value and real estate). We also see the results of an equal-weighted, annually rebalanced portfolio of the five indices (keep in mind the return advantages of small-cap stocks discussed earlier).

For the most recent 15-year period, BRK produced a 1.7 percentage point per year higher return than the S&P 500 Index and a 0.2 percentage point per year higher return than did the MSCI U.S. Prime Market Value Index. However, it produced a lower return than the other three indices, from 4.0 percentage points a year to 4.1 percentage points per year. The equal-weighted portfolio returned 8.5 percent per year, 2.1 percentage points per year higher than BRK's return.

We can see further evidence of the increasing difficulty of generating alpha by looking at the returns of two investors

Warren Buffett identified in his speech, "The Superinvestors of Graham-and-Doddsville." Buffett identified these investors in a talk he gave in 1984 in honor of the 50th anniversary of the publication of Benjamin Graham and David Dodd's book, *Security Analysis*. The two funds that Buffett mentioned in that speech with public records for the last 15 years are the Sequoia Fund and Tweedy Browne Value. We'll begin by looking at the returns of the legendary Sequoia Fund.

1999–2013

	15-YEAR ANNUALIZED RETURNS (%)
SEQUOIA FUND (SEQUX)	7.5
S&P 500 INDEX	4.7
MSCI US PRIME MARKET VALUE INDEX	6.2
MSCI US SMALL CAP 1750 INDEX	10.4
MSCI US SMALL CAP VALUE INDEX	10.5
DOW JONES US SELECT REIT INDEX	10.5
EQUAL-WEIGHTED INDEX PORTFOLIO	8.5

For the most recent 15-year period, Sequoia produced a 2.8 percentage points per year higher return than did the S&P 500 Index, and a 1.3 percentage points per year higher return than the MSCI U.S. Prime Market Value Index. It underperformed the other three indices by from

2.9 percentage points per year to 3.0 percentage points per year, although these do have the advantage of being small-cap stocks. The equal-weighted index portfolio returned 8.5 percent per year, 1.0 percentage points per year higher than Sequoia's return.

Recalling our discussion in Chapter 1, we can also examine Sequoia's results in terms of their factor exposures.[4] An analysis over this period shows that the fund benefitted from significant exposures to value and quality. The fund was slightly tilted to large cap stocks. Its exposure to market beta was low. And its exposure to momentum was negative. After accounting for those factors, the remaining alpha was actually -0.8 percent per year.

Interestingly, in the 15 years before that, alpha was a positive 3.8 percent per year. Outside of market beta, none of the factors had significant exposures. This is an example of how persistent alpha is so elusive. It could also be an illustration of the increased difficulty of stock picking over time.

We now turn to analyzing the performance of Tweedy Browne Value (TWEBX).

---

4. A convenient website is www.portfoliovisalizer.com/factor-analysis.

1999–2013

	15-YEAR ANNUALIZED RETURNS (%)
TWEEDY BROWNE VALUE FUND (TWEBX)	5.6
S&P 500 INDEX	4.7
MSCI US PRIME MARKET VALUE INDEX	6.2
MSCI US SMALL CAP 1750 INDEX	10.4
MSCI US SMALL CAP VALUE INDEX	10.5
DOW JONES US SELECT REIT INDEX	10.5
EQUAL-WEIGHTED INDEX PORTFOLIO	8.5

For the most recent 15-year period, TWEBX produced a 0.9 percentage point per year higher return than the S&P 500 Index. However, its return was lower than the returns of the other four indices. Specifically, its return was lower than the returns of the two value indices by 0.6 percentage points and 4.9 percentage points, respectively. The equal-weighted fund portfolio returned 8.5 percent per year, 2.9 percentage points per year higher than the return of TWEBX.

We can again examine TWEBX's returns by their factor exposures. We see a similar story as with SEQUX. The fund benefitted from significant exposures to value and quality. Size exposure was almost zero. The exposure to market beta was low. And the exposure to momentum was negative.

Once these exposures are accounted for, the annual alpha was -2.0 percent. TWEBX started in early 1994, so we cannot examine the prior 15 years as we did with SEQUX.

Perhaps, like Warren Buffett, these "superinvestors" have been burdened by the huge amount of assets they have under management. Or, perhaps, over time alpha has become harder to generate. Or, it might be a combination of both. Perhaps more importantly, just as with Buffett himself, a good portion of these funds' returns come from exposure to value and quality factors. While these exposures led to outperformance versus the S&P 500, that is beta and not alpha. In terms of capturing the incredible shrinking alpha, "The Superinvestors of Graham and Doddsville" have been less than super for at least the past 15 years. This evidence serves to highlight the benefits of passive investment strategies.

There are two additional important issues that we need to discuss. Both help explain why it is so difficult for active investors to persistently outperform appropriate risk-adjusted benchmarks. The first has to do with the nature of competition.

THE NATURE OF THE COMPETITION

As we alluded to earlier, the nature of competition in investing is very different than it is in one-on-one competitions, such as chess or tennis, where even small differences in skill can lead to large differences in outcomes. The following example will illustrate why this is a key issue.

At the peak of his career, Roger Federer was the greatest tennis player of his era. He won 17 Grand Slam titles. What is important to understand is that Federer's competition is made up of other *individual* players. In terms of individual skill, Andy Roddick had a better serve, Andy Murray had a better backhand, Fernando Gonzalez had a better forehand, Rafael Nadal had a better baseline game and was a superior player on clay, Radek Stepanek had a better net game and David Ferrer was faster. Yet, Federer was the better player.

The world of investing presents a different situation than the one that faced Roger Federer. Understanding the difference between the two helps explain why it is so difficult to persistently generate alpha. First, we need to understand how securities markets set prices.

Mark Rubinstein, professor of applied investment analysis at the University of California's Haas School of Business, provided the following insight in his 2001 paper, "Rational Markets: Yes or No? The Affirmative Case." He writes: "Each investor, using the market to serve his or her own self-interest, unwittingly makes prices reflect that investor's information and analysis. It is as if the market were a huge, relatively low-cost, continuous polling mechanism that records the updated votes of millions of investors in continuously changing current prices. In light of this mechanism, for a single investor (in the absence of inside information) to believe that prices are

significantly in error is almost always folly. Public information should already be embedded in prices."

Rubinstein's point is that the competition for an investment manager isn't other investment managers, but the *collective wisdom* of the market. The implication is: "The quest for market-beating strategy boils down to an information-processing contest. The entity you are competing against is the *entire* market and the accumulated information discovered by all the participants and reflected in prices."

In his paper, Rubinstein provided another way to think about the quest for superior investment performance: "The potential for self-cancellation shows why the game of investing is so different from, for example, chess, in which even a seemingly small advantage can lead to consistent victories. Investors implicitly lump the market with other arenas of competition in their experience." Rex Sinquefield, former co-chairman of Dimensional Fund Advisors, put it this way: "Just because there are some investors smarter than others, that advantage will not show up. The market is too vast and too informationally efficient." In other words, what is referred to as the "wisdom of crowds" makes the market a very difficult competitor.

While the competition for Federer is other individual players, the competition for investment managers is the entire market. It would be as if each time Federer stepped on the court, he faced an opponent with Roddick's serve, Murray's backhand, Gonzalez's forehand, Nadal's baseline game,

Stepanek's net game and Ferrer's speed. If that had been the case, Federer would not have produced the same results. In fact, he may never have won a single tournament.

The important message in this comparison is that the results of any game are more dependent on the *relative* skill of the competition rather than on the *absolute* skill of the individual. And as we have been discussing, in the investment world the competition is not only very tough, but is getting persistently tougher.

Having completed our discussion on how markets set prices, we now turn to the second issue that helps explain why it is so difficult for active investors to persistently outperform appropriate risk-adjusted benchmarks.

SUCCESSFUL ACTIVE MANAGEMENT CONTAINS THE SEEDS OF ITS OWN DESTRUCTION

While the efficient markets hypothesis provides us with the theoretical explanation for the lack of persistence in active management, we will now discuss why even the most successful funds contain the seeds of their own destruction. In fact, the more successful the fund is, the more likely it is that its outperformance will be fleeting.

Active fund managers know that the more a fund diversifies, the more it will look like, and perform similarly to, its benchmark index. A fund whose holdings parallel those of its benchmark is known as a *closet index fund*. Therefore, in order to have the greatest chance to outperform, a fund must concentrate its assets in a few stocks—which is why "focus" funds were created. Unfortunately, while a strategy built around owning just a few of a fund manager's best ideas is the most likely way to generate world-class returns, it is also the most likely way to end up at the bottom of the rankings list.

Let us look at how the mutual fund world works. A new fund is created, and it starts out with a small amount of assets under management. The fund managers are aware of the risks of being a closet index fund, and so they concentrate their fund's assets in just a few equities while complying with SEC rules on diversification, which do not allow a fund to have more than five percent of its assets in any one stock. The fund managers also know that the market for large-cap stocks is highly efficient in terms of information, and thus they may concentrate their research efforts in the less informationally efficient asset class of small-cap equities. The fund happens to be in the right place at the right time, or has one of the rare and truly gifted managers—perhaps the "next Peter Lynch"— and earns spectacular returns for a few years. The fund is given the coveted five-star rating from Morningstar and its managers start to advertise the fund's great performance. Assets come rushing in. The better the performance, the more cash flows into the fund. The fund managers are now faced with a dilemma. They must decide to either buy very large positions in just a very few small-cap stocks or they must increase the fund's diversification. The only other alternative is to style-drift to large-cap stocks. All three choices contain the seeds of the fund's likely inability to continue its record of outperformance. Let us see why this is the case.

If the fund starts to diversify, increasing the number of small-cap companies it owns, it runs into the inevitable math of becoming a closet index fund. A closet index fund looks like an actively managed fund on the surface, but the stocks it owns so closely resemble the holdings of a traditional index fund that investors are unknowingly paying very large fees for minimal differentiation. For example, if a fund is differentiated even as much as 50 percent from its benchmark index, the hurdle created by the operating expense ratio is almost twice the published figure. If the fund is only 20 percent differentiated, the hurdle becomes approximately five times the operating expense ratio. A relatively good indicator of the amount of differentiation in an actively managed fund is the fund's correlation with its benchmark index, such as the S&P 500 Index for large-cap stocks and the S&P 600 Index for small-cap stocks. The higher the fund's correlation coefficient—measured by a fund's r—the less the differentiation is likely to be. The fund's r-squared (the coefficient of determination) is commonly used to measure the degree of differentiation compared to a benchmark. The more the fund diversifies, the greater its r-squared becomes and the heavier the burden a fund manager carries in order to outperform. Add this burden to the others that actively managed funds and their investors must surpass (expenses such as bid/offer spreads,

commissions, market impact costs, the drag of cash and taxes for assets in taxable accounts) and the obstacles become much more insurmountable.

The following is evidence indicating the difficulty of overcoming a high r-squared figure, given the greater fees and other expenses incurred by active managers. A study found that for the three years ending Aug. 31, 1999, the five largest funds with r-squared figures over 95 returned between 21 percent and 26.9 percent. After taxes, an investor would have received between 18 percent and 24.6 percent. Vanguard's S&P 500 Index fund beat each of them. It returned 28.5 percent pre-tax and 27.5 percent after taxes. Of the 80 largest funds with r-squared figures over 95, only three managed to beat the Vanguard index fund before taxes, and they did so just barely. None of the funds did so after taxes.

The second alternative to dealing with the substantial cash inflow to our currently outperforming mutual fund is to continue concentrating assets in those same few stocks that made the fund successful in the first place. Here, the fund runs into a problem with market impact costs. Market impact is what occurs when a mutual fund wants to buy or sell a large block of stock. The fund's purchases or sales will cause the stock to move beyond its current bid (lower) or offer (higher) price, increasing the cost of trading. MSCI Barra, a market research organization, has studied market impact costs extensively. While market impact costs will vary depending on many factors (such as fund size, asset class and turnover) they can be quite substantial. MSCI Barra noted that a fairly typical small-cap or mid-cap stock fund with $500 million in assets and an annual turnover rate of between 80 percent and 100 percent could lose 3 percent to 5 percent per year to market impact costs—far more than the annual expenses of most funds. Because of their lack of liquidity, the smaller the market cap of the equities in a fund, the greater that fund's market impact costs can be. And the larger the amount of assets in a fund, the greater its total market impact costs can become.

The third alternative to dealing with an inflow of cash to our successful mutual fund is to style drift to larger-cap stocks. This is the alternative course of action that many funds will follow. The problem here is that the larger the market cap of an equity, the more efficient the market is informationally. This makes it extremely difficult to outperform.

No matter which way the manager turns, the likelihood of continued outperformance diminishes. The best option for a fund may be to stay small in terms of its assets under management. This can be accomplished by closing the fund to new investors. The problem is that not many funds are willing to forego the profits associated with increased assets under management—and further, a closed fund is of no use to new investors.

In a 2001 speech, "Three Challenges of Investing," Vanguard Group founder John Bogle discussed the results of his study on the encore performances of top-performing actively managed funds.[5] His findings support the theory that successful performance contains the seeds of its own destruction. Bogle compared the performance of the top 20 funds for the period 1972–1982 with their performance for the period 1982–1992. He found that the top 20 funds did perform slightly better in the second period than the average active fund, finishing in the 54th percentile. However, the margin of outperformance fell from 8.3 percent to just 1.2 percent. More importantly, they *underperformed* the S&P 500 Index by 1.8 percent. And that is before considering any loads or the impact of taxes. What is more, the dispersion of returns in the succeeding period was huge—the new rankings ranged anywhere from two to 245 (out of 309). Investors might have gotten lucky, or they may have paid a big price. There was no way to know before the fact.

Bogle found a similar story when he examined returns for the periods 1982–1992 and 1992–Sept. 30, 2001. The top 20 performers from the first period finished the succeeding period with an average ranking at the 58th percentile. However, the average outperformance fell from 4.9 percent to just 0.9 percent. More importantly, they *underperformed* the S&P 500 Index by 1.5 percent. Again, this is before considering any loads or the impact of taxes. Also, once again, there was a wide dispersion of returns—rankings in the succeeding period ranged from 14 to 823 (out of 841).

---

5.   http://www.vanguard.com/bogle_site/sp20011021.html

There is yet another problem for investors seeking the Holy Grail of outperformance. Since it takes time before a manager can demonstrate top performance, most of the outperformance will likely occur when the fund's assets are small. Thus, few shareholders actually earn the great returns. Most fund assets pile in only *after* great returns are earned. By the time the fund's performance reverts to the mean—which is what the evidence suggests is highly likely to occur—most of its invested dollars may well have earned below market returns. This can occur despite the fund's ability to show high annualized returns buoyed by its early outperformance. This is consistent with the evidence on investment behavior and returns. By chasing yesterday's performance, investors earn rates of return well below those of the very funds in which they invest. They tend to buy high (after great performance) and sell low (after poor performance). Not exactly a prescription for successful investing.

Before concluding this section, it is worth considering the case of Peter Lynch, generally considered the greatest mutual fund manager of them all. Lynch joined Fidelity in 1966. However, it was not until 1977 that he was given responsibility for the Magellan Fund, which was not even available to the public until mid-1981. Prior to that time, it operated as the private investment vehicle of the Johnson family, Fidelity's founders. From mid-1981 through mid-1990, Lynch outperformed the S&P 500 Index by 6 percentage points per year (22.5 percent versus 16.5 percent). Lynch started with about $100 million under management, but ended up running $16 billion. The original small-cap fund not only had become a large-cap fund, but it also eventually owned 1,700 stocks. While Lynch did generate alpha, even over the latter part of his reign, the size of his outperformance deteriorated, just as we should expect. Over the last four years, Magellan managed to beat the S&P 500 Index by about 2 percent per year. Still a great performance, although not quite as legendary—and one that might be explained by random good luck. Perhaps Lynch purposely retired from managing the fund in 1990 before the game was up and market forces caught up with him. He may have recognized that—because of the market's efficiency and hurdles to outperformance made higher by closet indexing, market impact costs and the other burdens of active management—the odds of his continuing success were not very good. Why not go out on top? While we will never know how Lynch would have done if he had continued to run Magellan, his carefully handpicked successors all failed to deliver alpha.

There is yet one more risk for investors in actively managed funds. The next "Peter Lynch"—whose stock-picking skills you were relying upon for returns—may decide to leave the fund to set up his own hedge fund, where he gets paid a lot more. Now what is the shareholder to do? The problem is compounded if the fund is held in a taxable account, and taxes would be owed on any realized gain. Investors in passively managed funds never have to worry about such potential situations.

It is important that we note that while active investors are not likely to persistently generate alpha, they do provide important societal benefits.

THE BENEFITS PROVIDED BY ACTIVE INVESTORS

Active managers play an important societal role—their actions determine security prices, which in turn determine how capital is allocated. And it is the competition for information that keeps markets highly efficient both in terms of information and capital allocation. Passive investors are "free riders." They receive all the benefits from the role that active managers play in making the financial markets efficient without having to pay their costs. In other words, while the prudent strategy is to be a passive investor, we don't want everyone to draw that conclusion. Passive investors need hope to spring eternal for those still convinced active management is the winning strategy.

We now turn our attention to the interesting question of whether or not the stock market has become overgrazed.

CHAPTER 3
IS THE MARKET OVERGRAZED?

In a May 2014 study, Claude Erb asked the question: Is the market overgrazed? Erb begins by noting that, over time, the market beta, size and value premiums have all declined, and are now at lower levels than their historical averages. The exception is the premium for small value stocks. He then asked: "What if too many investors are demanding too much from a possibly limited supply of opportunities?" Said another way, are the "trades" too crowded? Erb explained why he believes this has happened.

"Empirical research over the last fifty years has produced much awareness of past asset returns." He added: "Empirical academic research breeds familiarity with previously successful investment opportunities" and "familiarity breeds investment."

The June 2014 study, "Does Academic Research Destroy Stock Return Predictability," by David McLean and Jeffrey Pontiff provides support for Erb's thesis. The authors found that the average characteristic's return has a "56% post-publication decay." They also found that "strategies concentrated in stocks that are more costly to arbitrage have higher expected returns post-publication. Arbitrageurs should pursue trading strategies with the highest after-cost returns, so these results are consistent with the idea that publication attracts sophisticated investors." All of this raises the question of whether or not the markets have been overgrazed. Declining premiums, at least, raise the suspicion that they have.

What is the implication for investors? If a trade or strategy is going to get crowded, you want to be there before it happens because you will benefit from investors driving prices in your favor. But there is a reason for the adage among investment professionals that you don't want to be a member of a crowd. When an investment strategy gets "crowded," due to large inflows from investors chasing returns, it is time to exit. Think of the recent bubble in residential real estate, the 1990s tech bubble, the "tronics" bubble of the 1960s and all the other bubbles that have occurred.

William Bernstein, author of the mini-book, *Skating Where the Puck Was,* demonstrated the wisdom of this adage. He examined the returns of hedge funds, applying a three-factor analysis to the Hedge Fund Research Global Returns series for the period from 1998 through 2012. Bernstein found that while hedge funds did produce large alphas in the first third of the period, as investor assets chased those returns alpha shrank, and then turned negative.

From 1998 through 2002, the hedge funds produced an incredible alpha of 9.0 percent. However, from 2003 through 2007, their alphas went to -0.7 percent. And from 2008 through 2012 the alpha became -4.5 percent. As shown in the table below, the performance of hedge funds for the 10 calendar years 2004-2013 has been so bad that, in returning just 1 percent per year, they managed to underperform every major asset class, including virtually riskless one-year Treasuries.

2004-2013
ANNUALIZED RETURNS (%)

HFRX GLOBAL HEDGE FUND INDEX	1.0
DOMESTIC INDICES	
S&P 500	7.4
MSCI US SMALL CAP 1750 (GROSS DIVIDENDS)	10.4
MSCI US PRIME MARKET VALUE (GROSS DIVIDENDS)	7.4
MSCI US SMALL CAP VALUE (GROSS DIVIDENDS)	9.4
DOW JONES SELECT REIT	8.2
INTERNATIONAL INDICES	
MSCI EAFE (NET DIVIDENDS)	6.9
MSCI EAFE SMALL CAP (NET DIVIDENDS)	9.5
MSCI EAFE SMALL VALUE (NET DIVIDENDS)	10.1
MSCI EAFE VALUE (NET DIVIDENDS)	6.8
MSCI EMERGING MARKETS (NET DIVIDENDS)	11.2
FIXED INCOME	
MERRILL LYNCH ONE-YEAR TREASURY NOTE	2.1
FIVE-YEAR TREASURY NOTES	4.3
20-YEAR TREASURY BONDS	6.1

Where did the alpha go? What made it disappear? Did these masters of the universe suddenly lose their mojo? David Hsieh, professor of finance at Duke University's Fuqua School of Business, provided a simple explanation. Alpha is a finite resource.

Hsieh, who is engaged in ongoing research on the hedge fund industry, presented his findings at the CFA Institute's February 2006 hedge fund conference. He told listeners at the conference that he was comfortable concluding there was a finite amount of available alpha for the entire hedge fund industry—roughly $30 billion each year. The implication is that as more money enters the industry, there is less and less alpha per hedge fund to go around. This wasn't good news for hedge fund investors, because dollars had been flowing in at a rapid pace.

While we have no way of knowing how Hsieh determined his $30 billion figure, let us assume that his estimate was correct. We can now determine what that means for hedge fund investors. Hsieh estimated that, at the time, the industry had about $1 trillion under management. Approximately $30 billion of alpha spread over $1 trillion of assets is roughly 3 percent alpha for the entire industry. Of course, that is gross alpha, and 3 percent doesn't go very far with standard hedge fund fees of 2% of assets under management plus 20% of any alpha.

Again assume that there is a finite amount of alpha, and it is $30 billion. Let us go back in time to when the hedge fund industry had just $300 billion under management. Then the industry-average alpha would have been 10 percent. That is close to the 9 percent alpha Bernstein calculated for the period 1998-2002. Investors would have received above-benchmark returns, and then poured more money into hedge funds. As a result, the available alpha became diluted. Despite their poor performance since 2002, total hedge fund assets under management have continued to grow. Today, the industry has assets of almost $3 trillion. And the news gets even worse. The very act of exploiting market mispricings makes them disappear, shrinking the available alpha over time as anomalies are uncovered and exploited. The result is an industry where more dollars are chasing fewer opportunities to generate alpha. Not a good prescription for investors seeking alpha.

The lesson here is that whenever an investment strategy that is supposedly exploiting some market mispricing has become popular, it may already too late to join the party. And when a strategy becomes popular, not only will it have low expected returns due to crowding, but the assets in it are now "weak hands"—the investors who tend to panic at the first sign of trouble. That leads to the worst returns occurring at the worst times, when the correlations of all risky assets move toward one.

So, is there any good news? Yes! Investors now have access to low-cost, transparent, structured portfolios that systematically capture, or harvest, return premiums. That means shrinking alpha doesn't necessarily mean lower returns, just lower costs for investors seeking exposure to these strategies. Investors profit from being able to diversify their portfolios across more low-correlating sources of returns without high costs that can more than offset the benefits.

Low-cost, structured funds not only can provide investors with exposure to small-cap and value stocks, but to the momentum and profitability factors as well. There are even low-cost, structured funds that provide access to products once considered squarely within the realm of the hedge fund world, such as commodities, the carry trade, shifting maturity bond strategies, low market beta stocks, low liquidity stocks and merger and convertible bond arbitrage.

A good example of how a "hedge fund strategy" can be implemented in a structured, low cost manner is with managed futures. Managed futures are basically trend-following strategies that can be accessed with passive strategies. Equity market neutral strategies are another example of a hedge fund strategy that can be replicated by going long on value stocks and short on growth stocks, or long on positive momentum stocks and short on negative momentum stocks. And these strategies can be implemented in a relatively low-cost, passive manner. They are also strategies that have provided positive long-term returns while exhibiting low correlation with more traditional stock and bond investments. Thus, you no longer need to hire a hedge fund and pay them 2-and-20 to incorporate any of these strategies into an investment plan. And you certainly don't need to hire what Yale's chief investment officer, David

Swensen, called a cancer on the institutional fund world—a fund of hedge funds—which typically charge an additional 1-and-10.

Before anyone jumps into these types of strategies, it is important to note that while an investment strategy may appear appealing on paper, once implementation costs are considered the real world returns sometimes don't look as good. This is especially true of strategies that have high turnover, such as momentum strategies. It is important to be sure that the fund manager you employ to implement the strategy is strongly skilled in building fund construction rules and controlling trading costs and operational risks.

We now turn our attention to the question: If markets can be overgrazed, can passive investing become overgrazed as well?

WHAT IF EVERYONE INDEXED?

To begin to answer the question, it is important to understand that we are a long way from that happening. Perhaps 40 percent of institutional assets and 15 percent of individual assets are invested in passive strategies. In addition, there will always be some trading activity from the exercise of stock options, estates, mergers and acquisitions, etc. With that in mind let us address the issue of the likelihood of active managers either gaining or losing an advantage as the trend toward passive management marches on.

We begin by addressing the issue of information efficiency. The proponents of active management argue that with less active management activity there will be fewer professionals researching and recommending securities, making it easier to gain a competitive advantage. This is the same argument they currently make about those "inefficient" small-cap and emerging markets. Unfortunately, their underperformance against proper benchmarks has been just as great in these asset classes. The reason is that less efficient markets are characterized by lower trading volumes, resulting in less liquidity and greater trading costs. As more investors move to passive strategies it may have been logical to conclude that trading activity would decline. Yet, despite the shift to passive management by both individuals and institutions, trading volumes have not declined, and in fact have set new records as the remaining active participants became become more active—think of all those high frequency traders. However, if investors shifting to passive management caused trading activity to fall, then liquidity would decline and trading costs would rise. This increase in trading costs would raise the already substantial hurdle that active managers have to overcome. Based on the evidence we have from the "inefficient" small-cap and emerging markets, any information advantage gained by a lessening of competition would be offset by an increase in trading costs. Remember that the costs of implementing an active strategy must be small enough that market inefficiencies can be exploited, after expenses.

In other words, the math is irrefutable. Passive investing doesn't win because active managers are dumb. And as John Bogle points out with his Costs Matters Hypothesis, you don't need the markets to be efficient for passive investing to be the winning strategy.[6] It is simple math. It is their greater costs that are the cause of their underperformance.

There is another interesting conclusion that can be drawn about the trend towards passive investing. Remember that for active managers to win, they must exploit the mistakes of others. It seems likely that those abandoning active management in favor of passive strategies are investors that have had poor experience with active investing. The reason this seems logical is that it doesn't seem likely that an individual would abandon a winning strategy. The only other logical explanation we can come up with is that an individual simply recognized that they were lucky. That conclusion would be inconsistent with behavioral studies that all show individuals tend to take credit for their success as skill based and attribute failures to bad luck. Thus, it seems logical to conclude that the remaining players are likely to be the ones with the most skill. Therefore, we can conclude that as the "less skilled" investors abandon active strategies, the remaining competition, on average, is likely to get tougher and tougher. As the trend to passive investing marches on there will be fewer and fewer victims to exploit, leaving the

---

6. http://www.vanguard.com/bogle_site/sp2004AIMRefficientMrkts.html

remaining active managers to trade against themselves. And that is a game that in aggregate they cannot win.

CHAPTER 4
WHAT YOU CAN DO

Those readers who watched too many old science fiction movies may recognize the reference in our title to the 1957 classic, "The Incredible Shrinking Man." In that film the protagonist begins shrinking, eventually becoming microscopic and undetectable to people. At the end of the movie he proclaims: "My fears melted away. And in their place came acceptance. All this vast majesty of creation, it had to mean something. And then I meant something too... I still exist!" So, can we accept the fact that the ability to generate alpha is persistently shrinking? And since the ability to generate alpha is very difficult to identify before the fact, what can one do?

Generating alpha is so difficult, that Charles Ellis called active management's quest for it the loser's game. The reason is not that it is impossible to generate alpha. Instead, it is that focusing your efforts on trying to find alpha is highly unlikely to prove productive. Thus, the prudent decision is to abandon the quest and play the winner's game. Instead of focusing your efforts on generating alpha, you should focus on the four critical things you can actually control:

1. What risks do you want to take—what asset classes and factors do you want exposure to—and how much exposure should you have to each?

2. Diversifying the risks you take sufficiently to minimize idiosyncratic (uncompensated) risks.

3. Invest only in passively managed vehicles. By that we mean funds whose construction rules are evidence-based (as opposed to being based on opinions), transparent, and implemented in a systematic way.

4. Keep all of your costs low, including fees and taxes.

1. WHAT RISKS TO TAKE AND HOW MUCH OF THEM?

All investing involves risk. Even the so called risk-free rate, while offering no absolute loss, can fall short of inflation and leave you with reduced purchasing power. And greater risk should come with greater expected return. However, this greater return is only expected, not guaranteed—otherwise it would not really be a risk. Thus, a crucial task is determining which risks to take and how much of them.

One source of risk comes from the asset classes in which you choose to invest. Stocks are more risky than bonds— they are more volatile and suffer greater shortfalls. Stocks also tend to fail at the worst possible times, such as during recessions when your labor capital can be subject to increased risk. However, over time this equity risk has compensated those who can bear it with greater returns. Similarly bonds have outperformed cash. You should also invest across different regions of the world. Here again emerging markets offer greater risk and greater potential reward than more developed economies. In addition, they diversify economic and geopolitical risks.

As we have argued in this book, another source of risk comes from the factors in which you invest. We believe that before investing in a factor the evidence should be both persistent and pervasive. That is, factors should work across extended time periods, across economic regimes, and in a variety of countries and types of assets. For example, we would expect small and value stocks to continue their historical outperformance because they have been effective in the U.S. since at least 1927 and worked across multiple countries and regions as well. Similarly, momentum and quality have been gaining greater acceptance. And newer factors such as low volatility, betting against beta, and investments are being rigorously tested and may be worth considering.

Not only must you decide which risks to take, but also how much. There is a great temptation to say you want high returns and thus load up on higher-risk assets. However, you should be confident that you are capable of bearing the associated risks. Those who sell off when a factor is underperforming all-too-often end up buying high and selling low. Thus, setting an appropriate long term allocation, one you are willing to live with through good and bad times, is a necessary condition for investment success.

2. DIVERSIFY YOUR RISKS

Deciding which risks to take is only part of what is needed to play the winner's game. The risks you choose must then be combined into a portfolio. Building an appropriate portfolio means avoiding idiosyncratic risk—risk from concentrated holdings which can be avoided through diversification. By choosing an appropriate amount of complementary positions—ones that tend to zig while others zag—you can balance the various risks and produce a portfolio allocation that is tailored to your unique ability, willingness and need to take risk. Thus, diversification means not just differing sets of returns during good times, but also adequate downside protection during bad times.

Diversification has been called the one free lunch in investing. Thus, we suggest that you eat as much of it as you can. Rather than trying to pick stocks or funds that will provide alpha, instead focus on the underlying drivers of their returns and how they fit together.

3. INVEST IN PASSIVELY MANAGED FUNDS

There are a variety of passively managed funds that provide exposure to these asset classes and factors. While many of these are index funds, passive does not necessarily have to mean indexed. Well-designed passively managed funds not only have the ability to provide deeper exposure to desired factors than commercially available indices, but they can minimize, or avoid, exposure to the negatives of indexing. Among the negatives of indexing are:

- **Sensitivity to risk factors varies over time.** Because indices typically reconstitute annually, they lose exposure to their asset class (or factors, such as market beta, size, value, momentum and profitability) over time as stocks migrate across asset classes during the course of a year.

- **Forced transactions can result in higher trading costs.** Accepting the risk of tracking error also allows structured funds to engage in patient trading strategies such as using algorithmic trading programs. Patient trading also provides opportunities to "sell liquidity" and earn a premium by purchasing stock at a discount. The opportunities arise (specifically in small- and especially micro-cap stocks) from the desire of active investors to quickly sell more stock than the market can absorb at the current bid. This can be a large benefit during periods of crisis, as long as the fund itself is not subject to investors fleeing the fund in a panic.

- **Risk of exploitation through front-running.** Active managers can exploit the knowledge that index funds must trade on certain dates.

- **Inclusion of all stocks in the index.** Research has found that very low-priced ("penny") stocks, extreme small growth stocks, stocks in bankruptcy, and IPOs have poor risk-adjusted returns. A structured portfolio could exclude such stocks using a simple filter.

- **Limited ability to pursue tax-saving strategies, including avoiding intentionally taking any short term gains and offsetting capital gains with capital losses.** Excluding REITs also improves tax efficiency.

- **Lowered ability to preserve qualified dividends.** A fund must own the stock that earns the dividends for more than 60 days of a prescribed 121-day period. That period begins 60 days prior the ex-dividend date.

- **Inability to limit securities lending revenue to the expense ratio.** When lending securities, otherwise qualified dividends become non-qualified, losing their preferential tax treatment.

However, from a tax perspective, securities lending revenue can be first used to offset the expense ratio of the fund. For taxable investors, the added tax burden could outweigh the extra income. Tax-managed structured funds can explicitly take this into consideration.

· **Inability to screen for other factors.** There are passively managed small and value funds that have successfully been using momentum screens, incorporating them into their fund construction strategies thus allowing them to avoid buying stocks that fall into their buy range, but are exhibiting negative momentum.

4. KEEP YOUR COSTS LOW

One thing you can certainly control is costs—the less you pay the more you keep. The most obvious component of costs is the overall fees charged by funds. This includes not only the management fee, but other expenses such as for marketing and loads when you buy or sell the fund. Indeed research has shown that the best predictor of relative fund performance is the expense ratio. Funds which expend great effort in the quest for alpha tend to have higher fees. The lower fees of passive funds which avoid this doubtful task are the main reason for their superior performance.

Another set of costs comes from trading. These costs

include explicit costs such as commissions and spreads in the price at which one can buy or sell a security. Other trading costs are more implicit, and thus harder to measure. These costs include market impact, or the amount a security's price will move when you try to trade a large amount. For active funds with high turnover that accumulate large positions in a few stocks, these trading costs can be high indeed, providing another source of drag on returns.

Every April, we are reminded of another cost we wish to keep low—taxes. Passively structured funds with their lower turnover tend to be more tax efficient than their high turnover active counterparts. As noted earlier, active funds not only tend to lag passive ones, but they do even worse after taxes. And there are passively managed funds that specifically focus on earning the highest after-tax return (not minimizing taxes at the expense of lower after-tax returns). For asset classes such as bonds which tend to be less tax efficient, holding them in a tax-advantaged account such as an IRA or 401(k) can keep the tax bill down.

While costs should be kept as low as possible, as with everything in life, it is sometimes worth paying more for value received. Small-cap value or emerging markets funds tend to have higher fees than a large-cap U.S. fund, but offer exposure to diversifying factors with higher prospective returns. Rebalancing can incur not only transactions costs but taxes as well. However, it allows you to bring your portfolio to your desired risk and return target. Oscar Wilde defined a cynic as someone who knows the price of everything and the value of nothing. Don't be penny wise and pound foolish, but measure all costs against a realistic assessment of the potential benefit.

PUTTING IT TOGETHER

These basic steps should help you play the winner's game of focusing on what you can actually control. Setting an asset allocation with appropriate amounts of diversified risks in a low-cost manner is a huge step in moving away from the loser's game of desperately seeking alpha. But you should not just set it and forget it. Things change, markets move, your life evolves. Thus, passive investing does not mean do nothing. Monitoring, rebalancing and tax managing your portfolio are necessary.

Every day that the market is open, prices change and your asset allocation shifts. You shouldn't worry about small changes. However, over time they can become more substantial. Monitoring and occasional rebalancing, keeping in mind trading costs and taxes, allows you to keep your portfolio aligned with your targets and objectives. Remember that selling better performing assets and buying lower performers helps you buy low and sell high. And when markets are down, harvesting losses provides tax benefits.

Not only do markets change but so does your life, and with it your target allocation may shift. If any of your plan's underlying assumptions change, your plan should be altered to adapt to the change. Life altering events (a death in the family, divorce, a large inheritance or loss of job) can impact the asset allocation decision in dramatic ways. Thus, your asset allocation decisions should be reviewed whenever a major life event occurs.

Even market movements can lead to a change in the assumptions behind the investment policy statement (IPS) and portfolio's asset allocations. For example, a major bull market, like the one we experienced in the 1990s, lowered the need to take risk for those investors who began the decade with a significant accumulation of capital, providing the opportunity to "take chips off the table." At the same time, the rise in prices lowered future expected returns, having the opposite effect on those with minimal amounts of capital (perhaps just beginning their investment careers). The lowering of expected returns to equities meant that to achieve the same expected return investors would have to allocate more capital to equities than would have been the case had returns been lower in the past. The reverse is true of bear markets. They raise the need to take risk for those with significant capital accumulation while lowering it for those with little. A good policy is to review your plan, and its assumptions, at least annually.

While establishing and monitoring your investment plan can take some time, it is well worth the effort. However, skipping the quest for the incredible shrinking alpha can free up a lot of your time. The result is that instead of spending time on the pursuit of alpha, you will be able to spend your time on the "big rocks" in your life—be they time spent with your loved ones, on your faith, your education, your dreams, a worthy cause, teaching or mentoring others. And what's important to remember is that even if you are among the very few who are successful at generating alpha, the "price" of success may have been that you lost the far more important game of life.

CONCLUSION

Let us summarize what we've discussed. The goal of actively managed funds is to generate alpha—returns above the appropriate risk-adjusted benchmark. It is important to add that since the only way to generate alpha is to hold a different, less diversified portfolio than the benchmark, the expected alpha should be sufficient to compensate for the increased idiosyncratic risk active managers take by failing to fully diversify.

The bad news for today's investors seeking alpha is that they face four hurdles that are becoming ever more difficult to overcome. First, the pool of available alpha has been shrinking, because what once was alpha is now recognized as beta. Second, the pool of victims that active managers can exploit to generate alpha is getting smaller as unskilled and once-lucky investors abandon the quest for alpha and both individual and institutional investors persistently increase their allocations to passive strategies. Third, the level of competition is getting ever tougher as better data and technology are used by ever more skilled managers. And fourth, the amount of assets competing for the scarce resource is growing.

On the other hand, for individual investors who recognize that the quest for alpha is a loser's game, the trends are all favorable. These investors benefit from the intense competition among providers of passively managed or structured funds. And competition from the many providers of ETFs, with their lower costs, has been driving expense ratios persistently lower. There are now many index products with fees of basis points in the single digits. This trend to lower expenses is making passive investing even more of a winner's game. And that is contributing to a vicious circle for active investors. Lower costs are helping drive more investors to become passive, shrinking the pool of victims that can be exploited and raising the hurdles for the generation of alpha. Indeed, in the 2014 Berkshire Hathaway shareholder letter, Warren Buffett requested that the trustee for his estate invest 90 percent of assets "in a very low-cost S&P 500 index fund." The remaining 10 percent he advised to invest in short-term government bonds.

In a fitting end to our story of the incredible shrinking alpha, active fund manager Ted Arsonson of AJO Partners stated in a June 1998 interview with Barron's: "None of my clients are taxable. Because, once you introduce taxes... *active management probably has an insurmountable hurdle.*

We have been asked to run taxable money—and declined. The costs of our active strategies are high enough without paying Uncle Sam."

While it is a tragedy that the vast majority of investors unnecessarily miss out on market returns that are available to anyone adopting a passive investment strategy, the truly great tragedy is that they also miss out on the important things in life in pursuit of the Holy Grail of outperformance. Our fondest wish is that this book has led you to the winner's game in both investing and, far more importantly, life.

APPENDIX A
DOES INDEXING/PASSIVE INVESTING GET YOU AVERAGE RETURNS?

The 1973 publication of Burton Malkiel's *A Random Walk Down Wall Street* set off a revolution. Malkiel presented findings from academic research on the failure of actively managed funds to beat the market. The standard response at the time was, "So what, you can't buy an index fund." That was true until John Bogle came along.

Bogle graduated from Princeton in 1951. His senior thesis was entitled: "Mutual Funds can make no claims to superiority over the Market Averages." In his 2010 book, *Don't Count On It*, Bogle recounted that his inspiration for starting an index fund came from three sources, all of which confirmed his 1951 research: Paul Samuelson's 1974 paper, "Challenge to Judgment"; Charles Ellis' 1975 study, "The Loser's Game"; and Al Ehrbar's 1975 *Fortune* magazine article on indexing. In 1974, Bogle founded The Vanguard Group, now the largest mutual fund company in the United States. He started the First Index Investment Trust, later renamed the Vanguard 500 Index

Fund, in December 1975. The following June, a very prescient story appeared in *Fortune*: "Index Funds: An Idea Whose Time is Coming." It concluded: "Index funds now threaten to reshape the entire world of money management."

Philosopher Arthur Schopenhauer said that all great ideas go through three stages. In the first stage, they are ridiculed. In the second stage, they are strongly opposed. In the third stage, they are considered to be self-evident. This was certainly the case for Bogle's experiment. When it was launched, his index fund was heavily derided by the mutual fund industry. The fund was even described as "un-American," and it inspired a widely circulated poster showing Uncle Sam calling on the world to "Help Stamp Out Index Funds." The fund was lampooned as "Bogle's Folly." Fidelity's chairman, Edward Johnson, assured the world that the company had no intention of following Bogle into index funds when he stated: "I can't believe that the great mass of investors are going to be satisfied with receiving just average returns. The name of the game is to be the best." Another fund manager, National Securities and Research Corp., categorically rejected the idea of settling for average. "Who wants to be operated on by an average surgeon?" they asked.

And that refrain—that indexing and passive investments in general will get you only average returns—became one of the big lies told by Wall Street.

Morningstar ranks funds by returns within each of the categories they consider. The table below shows the Morningstar percentile rankings for select passively managed funds from Vanguard and Dimensional Fund Advisors (DFA) for the 10- and 15-year periods ending October 31, 2014. Vanguard is the leading provider of index funds. DFA's funds are passively managed, but with the exception of their U.S. Large Fund, they are not index funds. When reviewing the rankings, keep in mind that they contain survivorship bias. Funds that have done poorly often disappear, either because investors fled and the fund was closed or the fund family merged the poorly performing fund into a better performing fund. Those poorly performing funds disappear from the rankings over time. As a result, the actual performance ranking of surviving funds is significantly understated. The longer the period, the worse the survivorship bias becomes because more funds have gone to the mutual fund graveyard.

Vanguard researched the problem of survivorship bias in a study that covered the period from 1997 through 2011.[7] They found that just 54 percent of the funds managed to even survive the full 15 years. The rest (2,364 funds) were either liquidated or merged into another fund in the same fund family, in some cases more than once.

John Bogle, the legendary founder of the Vanguard Group also studied this issue.[8] He found that about 7 percent of mutual funds "died" each year between 2001 and 2012.

7. "The mutual fund graveyard: an analysis of dead funds," https://personal. vanguard.com/pdf/s362.pdf

8. http://money.usnews.com/money/personal-finance/mutual-funds/ articles/2013/06/10/are-there-too-many-mutual-funds

Finally, consider this evidence from a study by Lipper, Inc. In 2003, 870 U.S. mutual funds were merged into other funds, and 464 were liquidated—1,334 funds had their records magically erased. In 2002, the pace was similar, with 839 mergers and 555 liquidations, for a total of 1,394 what we might call "mercy killings." And 2001 saw 956 mergers and 433 liquidations, for a total of 1,389 "executions." Not only was the death rate amazingly persistent, but that is a three-year total of 4,117 funds that went out of existence. Think about that figure and compare it to the total of 7,596 mutual funds that were available to investors at the end of 2012.

MORNINGSTAR PERCENTILE RANKING
(AS OF OCTOBER 31, 2014)

DOMESTIC FUND	10 YEARS	15 YEARS
VANGUARD 500 INDEX (VFINX)	29	50
DFA U.S. LARGE (DFUSX)	24	48
VANGUARD VALUE INDEX (VIVAX)	36	64
DFA U.S. LARGE VALUE III (DFUVX)	7	6
VANGUARD SMALL CAP INDEX (NAESX)	14	59
DFA U.S. SMALL (DFSTX)	16	36
DFA U.S, MICRO CAP (DFSCX)	39	24
VANGUARD SMALL CAP VALUE INDEX (VISVX)	27	58
DFA U.S. SMALL VALUE (DFSVX)	30	20
VANGUARD REIT INDEX (VGSIX)	34	34
DFA REAL ESTATE (DFREX)	42	27

INTERNATIONAL FUND	10 YEARS	15 YEARS
VANGUARD DEVELOPED MARKETS INDEX (VTMGX)	40	46
DFA INTERNATIONAL LARGE (DFALX)	39	43
DFA INTERNATIONAL VALUE III (DFVIX)	18	11
DFA INTERNATIONAL SMALL (DFISX)	28	12
DFA INTERNATIONAL SMALL VALUE (DISVX)	1	7
VANGUARD EMERGING MARKETS INDEX (VEIEX)	31	47
DFA EMERGING MARKETS II (DFEMX)	22	40
DFA EMERGING MARKETS VALUE (DFEVX)	14	17
DFA EMERGING MARKETS SMALL (DEMSX)	4	12
AVERAGE VANGUARD RANKING	30	51
AVERAGE DFA RANKING	22	23

Note: A percentile ranking of 1 represents the best performance, 100 the worst.

For the seven Vanguard index funds, the average 10-year and 15-year rankings were 30 percent and 51 percent, respectively. Again, keep in mind the impact of survivorship bias on the long-term rankings. If survivorship bias were accounted for, it is highly likely that the 15-year ranking for the Vanguard funds would be well below 50 percent. As for the 13 passively managed DFA funds, the average 10-year and 15 year rankings were 22 percent and 23 percent, respectively. Outperforming 78 percent and 77 percent of the *surviving* funds is hardly an average performance. And if Morningstar accounted for survivorship bias, their rankings would almost certainly be considerably higher. It is also interesting to observe that the funds' highest rankings were in the very asset classes proponents of active management say are the most inefficient—international small and small value stocks and emerging market equities. In fact, DFA's international small value fund (DISVX) achieved a first percentile ranking over the most recent 10-year period. This comparison provides strong evidence against the argument that actively managed funds are likely to outperform in "inefficient" markets. In reality, that is just another myth that the mutual fund industry tries to perpetuate.

It is also important to note that the rankings are based on pre-tax returns. In most cases, index and other passively managed funds will be more tax efficient, due to their typically lower turnover. And ETF versions would further enhance the tax efficiency of index funds.

Given the evidence, it is pretty clear that passively managed funds don't get you average returns. They provide investors with *market* returns of the asset classes in which they invest, and by doing so they produce above-average returns for their investors.

APPENDIX B
ACTIVE MANAGEMENT: THE ODDS OF ACHIEVING PORTFOLIO ALPHA

An overwhelming body of evidence demonstrates that the odds against successfully choosing a mutual fund that will outperform its appropriate risk-adjusted benchmark are high enough that it is not prudent to even try. For example, Robert D. Arnott, Andrew L. Berkin and Jia Ye, authors of the 2000 study "How Well Have Taxable Investors Been Served in the 1980s and 1990s?" found:

- The average mutual fund underperformed its benchmark by 1.75 percent per year before taxes and by 2.58 percent on an after-tax basis.

- Just 22 percent of the funds beat their benchmark on a pre-tax basis. The average outperformance was 1.4 percent; the average underperformance was 2.6 percent. However, on an after-tax basis, just 14 percent of the funds outperformed. The average after-tax outperformance was 1.3 percent, while the average after-tax underperformance

was 3.2 percent. Thus, the risk-adjusted odds against outperformance are about 17:1.

Keep in mind these results were from the 1980s and 1990s. As we have discussed, today's competition would almost certainly make outperformance even more difficult. Worse still, these already abysmal odds do not present an accurate picture of all the obstacles facing active management, which makes the true chance of its success even less likely. Let us see why that is the case.

Since diversification of risk across asset classes is an important part of a prudent investment plan, most investors build portfolios using a variety of funds to provide them with the desired exposure. Consider an individual investor wanting exposure to the following range of equity asset classes:

- U.S.: large, small, small value, large value and real estate.

- International: large, small, small value, large value and emerging markets.

The investor, believing that active management is the winning strategy, would choose 10 funds, hiring the very best fund in each of the above 10 asset classes. This is the way the typical pension plan or endowment invests. However, the question such an investor should ask is not, "What are the odds that *each* of the funds individually will generate alpha?"

Rather, an investor should ask, "What are the odds that a *portfolio* of actively managed funds will generate alpha?" And that is a very different question.

We can estimate the odds that a portfolio composed of 10 equally-weighted actively managed funds, rebalanced annually, will successfully generate alpha. To simplify the mathematics, we need to make several assumptions:

- All funds have the same true alpha of negative 0.8 percent per year. This seems like a reasonable estimate based on evidence from studies on the performance of actively managed mutual funds. The after-tax alpha would be more negative.

- The standard deviation of each fund's annual alpha is 5 percent.

- Alphas are uncorrelated across funds and across years, though this is probably not realistic. Funds that follow similar strategies will probably have positively correlated alphas.

- The normal distribution is a reasonable approximation for the distribution of fund alphas.

Based on these assumptions, the probabilities that a portfolio will have a positive average alpha over various horizons are:

NUMBER OF YEARS	PROBABILITY OF POSITIVE ALPHA
1	0.306
2	0.237
3	0.190
4	0.156
5	0.129
6	0.108
7	0.090
8	0.076
9	0.065
10	0.055

To see how sensitive the data is to our inputs, we now assume that the standard deviation of annual alpha is 7 percent. The results are:

NUMBER OF YEARS	PROBABILITY OF POSITIVE ALPHA
1	0.359
2	0.305
3	0.266
4	0.235
5	0.210
6	0.188
7	0.169
8	0.153
9	0.139
10	0.127

As you can see, the results are indeed sensitive to our assumptions. We would get similar sensitivity if we changed the true alpha instead of its standard deviation.

While the previously mentioned study found that just 22 percent of actively managed funds outperformed their appropriate risk-adjusted benchmark on a pre-tax basis over the 1980s and 1990s, we see that the odds of a *portfolio* of actively managed funds doing the same are much lower. And the tables reflect the odds for only a 10-year period. Note how the odds get progressively worse as the time period increases.

For taxable investors, the story gets even worse—just 14 percent of actively managed funds outperformed in the 1980s and 1990s. The odds of a *portfolio* of actively managed funds generating positive after-tax alpha over the long term are surely much, much worse.

Moreover, the odds of outperformance would get progressively smaller as we increased the number of funds in the portfolio to add other asset classes, such as: fixed income assets (short- and long-term bonds, nominal and real, taxable and municipal, government and corporate, investment-grade and "junk" bonds), commodities and additional equity asset classes (international real estate, emerging markets, small and value).

It is also important to remember that most investors have investment horizons longer than 10 years. And the longer we extend the investment horizon, the worse the odds of success for active management.

The results produced by this simulation are supported by the 2013 study, "A Case for Index Fund Portfolios," by Richard A. Ferri and Alex C. Benke. Using live data from both index

and actively managed funds, they performed 5,000 simulated trials by randomly selecting actively managed funds from each asset class.

The authors first looked at the performance of a three-fund portfolio for the 16-year period 1997-2012. The index fund portfolio they used was allocated 40 percent to Vanguard Total Stock Market Index Fund Investor Shares (VTSMX), 20 percent to the Vanguard Total International Stock Index Fund (VGTSX) and 40 percent to the Vanguard Total Bond Market Index Fund (VBMFX). This portfolio outperformed 83 percent of the simulated active fund portfolios.

Using the Sharpe ratio as their measure, the authors also examined the risk-adjusted odds of a portfolio outperforming its benchmark. They found that the odds of success fell from about 17 percent to about 14 percent.

They also tested whether using more than one active fund in each asset class improved the odds of a portfolio's success. They found that using one active fund provided a 17 percent chance of outperformance while using two active funds in each asset class reduced the odds of success to just 13 percent. And using three active funds in each asset class reduced the odds to just 10 percent. It is important to note that the authors only examined pre-tax returns.

The authors then built a portfolio that consisted of 10 asset classes. Given the limited availability of index funds for each of the asset classes included, the study only covered the 10-year period 2003-2012. The study's index portfolio had

10 percent allocations to each of the following asset classes/ funds:

- Large-cap U.S. equity: Vanguard 500 Index Fund (VFINX)

- Mid-cap U.S. equity: Vanguard Mid-Cap Index Fund (VIMSX)

- Small-cap U.S. equity: Vanguard Small-Cap Index Fund (NAESX)

- Real estate (REITs): Vanguard REIT Index Fund (VGSIX)

- Developed international equity: Vanguard Developed Markets Index Fund (VDMIX)

- Emerging markets equity: Vanguard Emerging Markets Stock Index Fund (VEIEX)

- Short-term Treasury bonds: iShares Barclays 1-3 Year Treasury Bond Fund (SHY)

- U.S. investment-grade bonds: Vanguard Total Bond Market Index Fund (VBMFX)

- U.S. inflation-protected securities: iShares Barclays (TIP) (2004-2012), Vanguard Inflation-Protected Securities (VIPSX) (2003 only)

- Tax-exempt bonds: iShares S&P National AMT-Free Muni Bond Fund (MUB) (2008-2012),

Vanguard Intermediate-Term Tax-Exempt Fund
(VWITX) (2003-2007)

The authors found that the index fund portfolio outperformed actively managed portfolios in 90 percent of the simulations.

The research demonstrates that the main explanation for active management's failure to generate alpha is because of expenses, so the authors performed one other test. They screened out the half of the active funds with the highest expense ratios. For the three-fund portfolio, covering the 16-years 1998-2012, the odds of success did improve from 17 percent to 28 percent. That is still a 72 percent failure rate. And it is also pre-tax. Similar results occurred for the 10-fund portfolio covering the 10-year period 2003-2012. The odds of success rose from 10 percent to 29 percent. The failure rate was still 71 percent.

The conclusion we can draw from this research is that active management is the triumph of hype, hope and marketing over wisdom and experience. Choosing passively managed funds to implement your investment plan is the winning strategy, and the one most likely to allow you to achieve your goals.

APPENDIX C
THE VALUE OF SECURITY ANALYSIS

We have covered some of the reasons why active investors have such a difficult time achieving alpha. The following account provides further evidence into why the quest for this "Holy Grail" has generally proven fruitless.

The basic premise of active management is that, through their *efforts*, security analysts are able to identify and recommend, or buy, stocks that are undervalued and avoid stocks that are overvalued. The *result* will be that they, and investors following their recommendations, will outperform the market. But just how likely is it for the *efforts* of active managers to produce *results*?

In May 1999, at a conference for financial economists at UCLA's Anderson School of Management, Bradford Cornell presented a case to provide some insight into the value of the efforts of security analysts. Because much of the value of companies with high growth rates comes from distant cash flows, their stock is highly sensitive to the size of the equity risk premium (ERP)—the larger the ERP, the higher the rate used to discount the expected cash flows and the bigger the impact on the estimated value. The ERP is the premium above the rate on riskless Treasury instruments that investors demand in exchange for accepting the risks of equity ownership. In 1999, Intel was certainly considered a company expected to post a high rate of growth.

At the time, Intel had accumulated more than $10 billion in cash. The board of directors was trying to determine if it made sense to use a substantial portion of that cash to repurchase stock. At the time, the stock was trading at about $120 per share. Based on publicly available forecasts of future cash flows, Cornell demonstrated that if the ERP was 3 percent, Intel's stock would be worth $204. If the ERP was 5 percent, the stock would be worth $130, about the current price. And if the ERP was 7.2 percent, the stock would be worth just $82.

BUY, SELL OR HOLD

With such a wide range of estimated stock values, what should the board do? If the stock was indeed worth $204 per share, they should begin an aggressive repurchase program. On the other hand, if the stock was actually worth $82, they should take advantage of the current "overvaluation" and raise capital by issuing more shares. The board was faced with two problems. The first was that these valuations assumed the cash flow projections were a known fact. Not even the board, let alone some security analyst, can see the future with such clarity. Obviously, in the real world we can only make estimates of future cash flows. The second is that is there any reason to believe the board can predict the ERP any better than the market could? It is easy to see how much the stock valuation changes with changes in the ERP.

In hindsight, the board should have issued a lot more shares. Some 15 years later, in October 2014, Intel's stock price was only about one-fourth of the $120 per share it had been. If corporate insiders—e.g., a board of directors with access to far more information than any security analyst or investor is likely to possess—have such great difficulty in determining a "correct" valuation, it is easy to understand why the results of conventional stock-picking methods (active management) are poor and inconsistent. Security analysts, active portfolio managers and individual investors are expending a great amount of effort in their attempts to beat the market, but the historical evidence has shown those efforts to be counterproductive a majority of the time. Smart investors, like smart businesspeople, care about results, not effort. That is why "smart money" invests in passively managed portfolios.

APPENDIX D
THE PERFORMANCE OF ACTIVE MANAGERS IN BEAR MARKETS

One of the arguments often made in favor of investing in actively managed funds is that they outperform in bear markets. The reason cited for this performance is that, unlike index funds, actively managed funds have the ability to reduce their exposure to stocks by selling them as part of a move into cash or cash equivalents. If it is true that actively managed funds outperform in bear markets, it is possible that—even though actively managed funds underperform over the long term—some investors will be willing to trade off long-term underperformance for short-term outperformance in down markets. Unfortunately, the evidence demonstrates the assumption that actively managed funds outperform in bear markets is nothing more than yet another myth that the mutual fund industry attempts to perpetuate.

To test this hypothesis, Vanguard examined active fund returns for the period 1970-2008, and analyzed the seven periods in that time during which the Dow Jones Wilshire

5000 Index fell at least 10 percent and the six periods in that time during which the MSCI EAFE Index fell by at least that amount. The results were published in a 2009 issue of *Vanguard Investment Perspectives*. Despite acknowledging survivorship bias—poorly performing funds disappear and are not accounted for—Vanguard found:

- It doesn't matter whether an active manager is operating in a bear market, a bull market that precedes or follows a bear market, or across longer-term cycles. The costs arising from security selection and market timing prove to be a difficult hurdle to overcome.

- "Success" in a bear market can be explained, at least in part, by style exposures. For example, during the bear market of September 2000 through March 2003, the Russell 1000 Value Index fell just 21 percent while the U.S. total market lost more than 42 percent. Once active funds were compared to their style benchmarks, there was no consistent pattern of outperformance. Past success in overcoming this style exposure hurdle doesn't ensure future success. The degree of attrition among winners from one period to the next indicates that successfully navigating one, or even two, bear markets might be more strongly linked to simple luck than to skill.

Vanguard concluded: "We find little evidence to support the purported benefits of active management during periods of market stress."

Vanguard's conclusion is confirmed by Standard & Poor's finding in its 2008 *Indices Versus Active (SPIVA)* scorecard. Standard & Poor's concluded: "The belief that bear markets favor active management is a myth. A majority of active funds in eight of the nine domestic equity style boxes were outperformed by indices in the negative markets of 2008. The bear market of 2000 to 2002 showed similar outcomes."

As the evidence demonstrates, the belief that active managers are likely to protect investors from bear markets is just another myth propagated by Wall Street.

APPENDIX E
FOR ACTIVELY MANAGED FUNDS HOW LONG A TRACK RECORD IS ENOUGH?

Whenever the evidence on the failure of active management to persistently outperform is presented, the typical response from skeptics goes something like: "Who cares about the average fund? I only invest in funds with great long-term track records." The argument continues along these lines: "While a short-term record of beating the market might be luck, certainly a long-term record must be skill-based."

The problem with this line of thinking is that the studies on this subject have found no persistent outperformance beyond the randomly expected—the past is not prologue when it comes to mutual fund returns. In other words, given the huge number of active managers trying to beat the market, the odds are that some of them will randomly outperform, even over long time frames.

The following four examples demonstrate that even long track records of outperformance don't provide insight into future performance.

THE 44 WALL STREET FUND

Most investors would be surprised to learn that Peter Lynch, and the mutual fund he ran was not the top-ranked fund of the 1970s. Thanks to its now long-forgotten manager, David Baker, the 44 Wall Street Fund generated even greater returns than Lynch's Magellan Fund, making it the top-performing diversified U.S. stock fund of the decade. Surely, 10 years of achieving the best performance in an entire industry could not be the result of pure luck. Or, could it? How were investors rewarded for believing that past performance of active managers is prologue?

While the S&P 500 Index returned 17.6 percent per year— each $1 invested grew to more than $5—the 44 Wall Street Fund ranked as the single worst performing fund in the 1980s, losing 73 percent—each $1 invested turned into just 27 cents. The fund did so poorly that it was merged into the Cumberland Growth Fund in April 1993, which was then merged into the Matterhorn Growth Fund in April 1996.

We next consider the case of a fund that accomplished what even Peter Lynch never did—beat the S&P 500 Index for 11 years in a row.

THE LINDNER LARGE-CAP FUND

For each of the 11 years 1974-1984, the Linder Large-Cap Fund outperformed the S&P 500 Index. However, over the next 18 years, the S&P 500 Index returned 12.6 percent per year while the Lindner Large-Cap Fund returned just 4.1 percent—an underperformance of 8.5 percentage points per year. The Lindner Fund was finally put out of its misery when it was purchased by the Hennessy Funds in October 2003, and eventually merged into the Hennessy Total Return Fund.

Next up is the case of Bill Miller, who managed to beat the S&P 500 Index for 15 years in a row. Surely, that long a streak of excellence can be relied on to continue.

THE LEGG MASON VALUE TRUST FUND

By the end of 2005, Bill Miller's streak of outperforming the S&P 500 Index had reached 15 consecutive years. That streak was broken in 2006, when the fund underperformed the S&P 500 Index by about 10 percentage points. His 2007 performance was even worse, underperforming the S&P 500 Index by about 12 percentage points. And 2008 was even more miserable, as the fund underperformed that benchmark by about 18 percentage points. Miller finally reversed that performance in 2009, when his fund beat the S&P 500 Index by about 14 percentage points. Unfortunately, the fund underperformed the S&P 500 Index in 2010 by more than 8 percentage points. It again underperformed in 2011 by about 6 percentage points. In 2012, the reigns of the fund were handed over to a new manager.

There is one last case to present. Although it is not

about a mutual fund, it is a tale about relying on the past performance of active managers.

THE TIGER FUND

The Tiger Fund hedge fund was formed in 1980 by the legendary Julian Robertson, with $10 million in capital. The fund had a remarkable run, averaging returns of more than 30 percent per year for its first 18 years. By 1998, it had in excess of $22 billion under management—the vast majority coming from new investments. Over the next two years, however, The Tiger Fund stumbled badly, losing more than $10 billion. The fund closed its doors in March 2000. The irony is that, while the fund still shows a return of 25 percent per year over its lifetime, it is estimated that investors in the fund may have actually lost money. The reason is that most of the money came in late, after the great returns had already been earned.

These tales demonstrate that 10, 11, 15 or even 18 years of outperformance are simply not sufficient to draw reliable conclusions.

What always surprises me is that the same people who are concerned about their personal health, and thus heed the Surgeon General's warning about the dangers of cigarettes, will ignore the SEC warning that relying on the past performance of money managers is dangerous to your financial health.

APPENDIX F
THE Q-FACTOR MODEL

Kewei Hou, Chen Xue, and Lu Zhang, authors of the study "Digesting Anomalies: An Investment Approach," proposed a new four-factor model that went a long way to explaining many of the anomalies that neither the Fama-French three-factor, nor four-factor, models could explain. The study covers the period from 1972 through 2012.

The authors called their model the q-factor model. The four factors are:

- The market excess return (beta).

- The difference between the return on a portfolio of small-cap stocks and the return on a portfolio of large-cap stocks. The size factor earned an average return of 0.31 per month with a t-stat of 2.12.

- The difference between the return on a portfolio of low investment-to-assets stocks and the return on a portfolio of high investment-to-assets stocks. They explain: "Intuitively, investment predicts returns because given expected cash flows, high costs of capital imply low net present values of new capital and low investment, and low costs of capital imply high net present values of new capital and high investment." They noted that the investment factor is highly correlated (0.69) with the value premium, suggesting that this factor plays a similar role to that of the value factor. The investment factor earned an average return of 0.45 percent per month with a t-stat of 4.95.

• The difference between the return on a portfolio of high return on equity (ROE) stocks and the return on a portfolio of low return on equity stocks. "ROE predicts returns because high expected ROE relative to low investment must imply high discount rates. The high discount rates are necessary to offset the high expected ROE to induce low net present values of new capital and low investment." The ROE factor earned an average return of 0.58 percent per month with a t-stat of 4.81. They noted that the profitability factor has a high correlation (0.50) with the momentum factor—it plays a similar role as the momentum factor in analyzing performance.

Among their important findings was that the investment and profitability (ROE) factors are almost totally uncorrelated—they are independent, or unique, factors. In addition, they found that the alphas of the value and momentum factors in the q-factor model are small and insignificant. In other words, the value and momentum factors are no longer needed to explain the differences in returns of diversified portfolio as their roles have been replaced by the investment and ROE factors.

The authors also found that the q-factor model outperforms the Fama-French three- and four-factor models in its ability to explain most anomalies—most become insignificant at the 5 percent level of statistical significance. The authors explain: "Many anomalies are basically different manifestations of the investment and ROE effects."

Given the importance of the issue of data mining, it is important to note that the investment and ROE factors had t-stats of close to five—they are highly significant. And while the t-stat of the size factor was lower at just over 2, including it helps the q-factor model fit the average returns across the size deciles.

Finally, the authors acknowledge: "The q-factor model is by no means perfect in capturing all the anomalies." Like all models even the q-factor model is flawed. However, it does seem that this new model has advanced our understanding of how markets set prices.

FAMA AND FRENCH EXAMINE THE Q-MODEL

Professors Eugene Fama and Kenneth French, in a March 2014 paper, "A Five-Factor Asset Pricing Model" took a close look at a model similar to the q-factor model, to see if these new factors—investment and profitability—added explanatory power. In other words, if Fama and French knew in 1993 what they know today, which model would they have chosen? The following is a summary of their findings:

- While a five-factor (beta, size, value, profitability, and investment) model does not fully explain the cross-section of returns (there are still anomalies) it provides a good description of average returns.

- The model's main problem is its failure to explain the low average returns on small stocks that invest a lot despite low profitability. (The Fama-French three-factor model also has a problem explaining the poor performance of small growth stocks.)

- The performance of the model is not sensitive to the specifics of the way its factors are defined.

- A four-factor model that excludes the value factor captures average returns as well as any other four-factor model considered. A five-factor model (including value) does not improve the description of average returns from the four-factor model. The reason is that average return to the value factor (specifically the return of high book-to-market stocks minus the return of low book to market stocks, or HML) is captured by the exposures of the HML factor to other factors. Thus, in the five-factor model, HML is redundant for explaining average returns.

Fama and French did note that "the four-factor model that drops HML seems to be as good a description of average returns as the five-factor model, but the five-factor model may be a better choice in applications. Though captured by exposures to other factors, there is a large value premium in average returns that is often targeted by money managers." Thus, "in evaluating how investment performance relates to known premiums, we probably want to know the tilts of [the] portfolios toward [each of the] factors." They added that "for explaining average returns, nothing is lost in using a redundant factor." Importantly, they also found that the five-factor model performs well: "Unexplained average returns for individual portfolios are almost all close to zero."

Among their interesting findings were that "controlling for investment, value stocks behave like stocks with robust profitability, even though unconditionally value stocks tend to be less profitable." They also found that the value, profitability, and investment factors are negatively correlated with both the market and the size factor, providing important

information regarding potential benefits from portfolios that diversify exposures across factors.

Another interesting finding is that "by far the biggest problem" is the extremely low returns of small stocks with "the lowest profitability and highest investment." However, they found that this problem doesn't hold for large stocks with low profitability and high investment. Note that passive portfolios can benefit from this knowledge by simply screening out stocks with these characteristics.

We return to the question, knowing what they know today, which model would they choose? Fama and French concluded that since HML seems to be a redundant factor in the sense that its high average return is fully captured by its exposure to other factors, "in applications where the sole interest is abnormal returns... our tests suggest that a four-factor model that drops HML performs as well as (no better and no worse than) the five-factor model. But if one is also interested in measuring portfolio tilts toward value, profitability, and investment, the five-factor model is the choice."

Only time will tell if either Hou, Xue and Zhang's q-factor model or Fama and French's five-factor model will become a new workhorse asset pricing model. However, with Fama and French's endorsement, it does seem like a good possibility that one of them will. More work continues to be done on the ability of these factor models to explain anomalies. And with each new discovery, once again alpha becomes beta.

REFERENCES

1. Alberg, John, and Michael Seckler. 2014. "Misunderstanding Buffett." *Advisor Perspectives*, (August 12).

2. Arnott, Robert D., Andrew L. Berkin and Jia Ye. 2000. "How Well Have Taxable Investors Been Served in the 1980s and 1990s?" *Journal of Portfolio Management,* vol. 26, no. 4 (Summer):84-93.

3. Banz, Rolf W. 1981. "The Relationship Between Return and Market Value of Common Stocks." *Journal of Financial Economics*, vol. 9, no. 1:1-28.

4. Barber, Brad M., and Terrance Odean. 1999. "The Courage of Misguided Convictions." *Financial Analysts Journal*, vol. 55, no. 6 (November/December):41-55.

5. Barber, Brad M., and Guojun Wang. 2011. "Do (Some) University Endowments Earn Alpha?" Working paper (October).

6. Basu, Sanjoy. 1983. "The Relationship Between Earnings' Yield, Market Value and Return for NYSE Common Stocks." *Journal of Financial Economics*, vol. 12, no. 1:129-156.

7. Berk, Jonathan B., and Jules H. van Binsbergen. 2013. "Measuring Skill in the Mutual Fund Industry." Working paper (November).

8. Bernstein, William. 2012. *Skating Where the Puck Was*, Efficient Frontier Publications.

9. Bogle, John C. 2010. *Don't Count on It*, Hoboken, NJ: John Wiley and Sons.

10. Carhart, Mark M. 1997. "On Persistence in Mutual Fund Performance." *Journal of Finance*, vol. 52, no. 1 (March):57-82.

11. Ellis, Charles D. 1975. "The Loser's Game." *Financial Analysts Journal*, vol. 31, no. 4 (July/August):19-26.

12. Ellis, Charles D. 2014. "The Rise and Fall of Performance Investing." *Financial Analysts Journal*, vol. 70, no. 4 (July/August):14-23.

13. Erb, Claude. 2014. "Has The Stock Market Been "Overgrazed"?" Working paper (May).

14. Fama, Eugene F., and Kenneth R. French. 1992. "The Cross-Section of Expected Stock Returns." *Journal of Finance*, vol. 47, no. 2 (June):427-465.

15. Fama, Eugene F., and Kenneth R. French. 2010. "Luck versus Skill in the Cross-Section of Mutual Fund Returns." *Journal of Finance*, vol. 65, no. 5 (October):1915-1947.

16. Fama, Eugene F., and Kenneth R. French. 2014. "A Five-Factor Asset Pricing Model." Working paper (March).

17. Ferri, Richard, and Alex Benke. 2014. "A Case for Index Fund Portfolios." *Journal of Indexes*, vol. 17, no. 1 (January/February):18-29.

18. Frazzini, Andrea, David Kabiller and Lasse H. Pedersen. 2013. "Buffett's Alpha." Working paper (November).

19. Frazzini, Andrea, and Lasse H. Pedersen. 2014. "Betting Against Beta." *Journal of Financial Economics*, vol. 111, no. 1 (January):1-25.

20. Hou, Kewei, Chen Xue and Lu Zhang. 2014. "Digesting Anomalies: An Investment Approach." *Review of Financial Studies* (to appear).

21. Jegadeesh, Narasimhan, and Sheridan Titman. 1993. "Returns to Buying Winners and Selling Losers: Implications for Stock Market Efficiency." *Journal of Finance*, vol. 48, no. 1 (March):65-91.

22. Lee, Dwight, and James Verbrugge. 1996. "The Efficient Market Theory Thrives on Criticism." *Journal of Applied Corporate Finance* vol. 9, no. 1 (Spring):35-41.

23. Malkiel, Burton G. 1973. *A Random Walk Down Wall Street*, New York, NY: Norton.

24. Mauboussin, Michael J., and Dan Callahan. 2013. "Alpha and the Paradox of Skill." Credit Suisse report (July 15).

25. McLean, R. David, and Jeffrey Pontiff. 2014. "Does Academic Research Destroy Stock Return Predictability?" Working paper (June).

26. Mladina, Peter, and Jeffery Coyle. 2010. "Yale's Endowment Returns: Manager Skill or Risk Exposure?" *Journal of Wealth Management*, vol. 13, no. 1 (Summer):43-50.

27. Novy-Marx, Robert. 2013. "The Other Side of Value: The Gross Profitability Premium." *Journal of Financial Economics*, vol. 108, no. 1 (April):1-28.

28. Pastor, Lubos, Robert F. Stambaugh and Lucian A. Taylor. 2013. "Scale and Skill in Active Management." Working paper (August).

29. Rosenburg, Barr, Kenneth Reid and Ronald Lanstein. 1985. "Persuasive Evidence of Market Inefficiency." *Journal of Portfolio Management*, vol. 11, no. 3 (Spring):9-16.

30. Rubinstein, Mark. 2001. "Rational Markets: Yes or No? The Affirmative Case." *Financial Analysts Journal*, vol. 57, no. 3 (May/June):15-29.

31. Sebastian, Mike, and Sudhakar Attaluri. 2014. "Conviction in Equity Investing." *Journal of Portfolio Management*, vol. 40, no. 4 (Summer):77-88.

32. Sharpe, William F. 1991. "The Arithmetic of Active Management." *Financial Analysts Journal*, vol. 47, no. 1 (January/February):7-9.

33. Stambaugh, Robert F. 2014. "Investment Noise and Trends." Working paper (April).

34. Swedroe, Larry. 2011. *The Quest for Alpha: The Holy Grail of Investing*, Hoboken, NJ: John Wiley and Sons.

35. Wermers, Russ. 2000. "Mutual Fund Performance: An Empirical Decomposition into Stock-Picking Talent, Style, Transactions Costs, and Expenses." *Journal of Finance*, vol. 55, no. 4 (August):1655-1695.

CPSIA information can be obtained
at www.ICGtesting.com
Printed in the USA
FSOW02n0018170215
5204FS